Unprotected Sects
(The Secret Life of a Celibate Monk.)

Nathan Vanek
(Bramachari Hansraj)

Dedication/opening quote:

'Grasping at things can only yield one of two results: either the thing you are grasping at disappears, or you yourself disappear. It is only a matter of which occurs first.'

S.N.Goenka.

Unprotected Sects (The Secret Life of a Celibate Monk)
By Nathan Vanek (Bramchari Hansraj)
Published in Canada by Hansa-Imaging Inc.
1062 Scantlings Vancouver BC V6H 3N8

ISBN: 978-1-989442-13-5

Front cover from a painting by John F. Marok.

Contents

Not Hung Like My Dad

My dad was a judge in Toronto for a hundred-and-fifty years, sometimes referred to as 'a hangin' judge.' So I suppose it's fitting that he was, in fact, physically rather well-hung. I remember catching him naked once when I was quite young and the size of his penis made a big impression on me. It was huge. I was shocked and at the same time strangely proud to have a father with a dick the size of a mule's. However, I was also disappointed by the realization that mine was not nearly as impressive. I was even a little pissed off, excuse the expression. Since I had inherited some pretty lousy characteristics from the guy, you'd think I could've at least been blessed with an equally impressive cock. I was saddened by the realization that I was, in fact, not hung like my dad.

Not long before he died, I was unfortunate enough to have to hold dad up in front of a urinal. And I found myself as shocked by his clownishly small penis as I had been by its immensity so many years before. His most wonderful asset, in my mind, had become his most horrid liability, both visually and practically. The problem, as I saw it while holding my father up awkwardly, was if a large and proud penis like his could end up shrinking into something so small and shrivelled, what could I expect?

More importantly, if atrophy, lack of sexual activity, was the cause of such a change in its countenance, I was in real fucking trouble. That's because I've been celibate for most of my adult life.

This book is my story, a memoire, a journey that specifically deals with the role of sexuality in a spiritual aspirant's life. Some of the more graphic parts are totally and ridiculously gratuitous. Be that as it may, and it may be reprehensible, I like to think it's a relevant book. It's certainly a fiercely personal account and no doubt will be offensive to many for one reason or another; I do like to think it'll have some value going forward other than for my grand-kids, especially since I have none. It's not the whole story of course, but surely enough of it and, yeah, I know some will consider it far too much. During a time, however, when there's finally a relatively open discussion going on concerning sexism, sexual misconduct, harassment and abuse, I do feel my story and this book will find a voice.

Keep in mind, if you will, as you read with a well-trained eye, that in this book i've declared war on the comma. Because we have all suffered long enough under its incessant demands. You might say that I feel we shared a comma enemy and it was high time for someone to take a stand. Lastly, most names have been changed, muddled or mixed up in order to protect and/or confuse the heck out of certain people

Can't Say I Wasn't Warned

April, May or perhaps June, 1998. Moving back in with my aged parents was positively freakish. Following thirty years, including twenty-five years in India as a Buddhist monk and a bramachari yogi, staying even temporarily in their North Toronto condominium was a questionable decision. What was I thinking? In my own defense I can only say that it seemed my least horrible option at the time. It was of course a tremendous test of my meditation practice, one which I failed miserably.

Upon carting my one suitcase into the den, dad warned me to stay right away from his private filing cabinet. He told me exactly where to put my clothes, showed me where a blanket was that I could use while sleeping on the sofa. Then he repeated that the filing cabinet was off-limits before leaving the room. After carefully unpacking I wandered into the kitchen, absently reached into a jar for a cookie and then mom slapped my hand so hard I jumped off the ground. "NOT BEFORE DINNER!," she barked. When I reminded her that I was a forty-eight-year-old gentleman she simply said: "Doesn't matter to me buster."

The whole apartment smelled of cooked animals and stale cigarettes so I opened up the den's screen-door. Unfortunately, even tragically, a fly flagrantly flew right in. I didn't really take any notice of it but by the time the fly made its way to the kitchen all hell broke loose. My old mom began yelling and running around the place waving a large spoon. She was completely out of control. My dad began hollering: "SHUT THE DAMN DOOR! SHUT THE GOD-DAMNED SCREEN DOOR!" In India of course one fly in a room would not raise an eyebrow. In that apartment it was as if we had been descended upon by an apocalyptic plague of locusts. Mom kept wildly trying to swat the thing and hitting appliances instead. Dad kept repeating that it was a huge problem, a HUGE problem. I made my second mistake by pointing out that leprosy is a huge problem and that one fly is really more of a nuisance. Suffice it to say my comment was not well received. The situation was finally resolved, however, at the expense of the life of the fly and with a heart-felt promise by me to never ever ever open the screen-door again.

After dinner, which for me consisted of some totally over-cooked broccoli and mashed potatoes all smothered in thick processed cheese, I received a phone call informing me that my good friend Shakti had suddenly passed away. That was deeply disturbing news for more than one reason. Aside from the obvious shock of losing a friend, I was apparently the last person to have spoken to her, a conversation that would haunt me for quite some time.

I could hear my parents bickering in the other room before they shuffled off down the hall to play 'Bridge' at the apartment of some neighbours. So I lay down in the den on the sofa and obviously I kept looking over at the filing cabinet. Eventually, just as obviously, I got up and opened it. I spent the evening reading my parents' 'Last Will and Testimony', my dad's investment portfolio and a few other interesting papers. It was not really interesting but at that point I really didn't want to dwell on the implications of Shakti's death, our last conversation, and I totally wanted to do something forbidden by my folks.

Dad spent about an hour next morning trying to convince me to shave off my beard. He even demonstrated his electric shaver, which he also generously offered for my use. After that, he and my mom had one of their epic fights while I hid in the den. It amazed me how little had changed in all those years and it occurred to me that I had landed in a kind of hell. In spite of my best efforts I kept hearing Shakti's voice: "Leaving's not as easy as you may think, Hansraj".

In the late afternoon, on a pretext, I left the building. In the elevator, an old guy wearing only a pair of boxer shorts and sleeveless T-shirt, with unkempt white hair and a grin that was frighteningly too wide, invited me to join him for a sauna, which I respectfully declined. It felt so good to get outside. First I walked then hopped a bus and eventually took a subway right downtown.

Walking along Yonge Street as darkness fell was of course strange. It had been so many years before, another lifetime that I lived on that street. Some things had changed; much remained just as I remembered. 'Sam The Record Man' was there. 'Old Navy' was there, along with familiar crowds, grittiness. I wandered into 'The Brass Rail.' I have no idea why except that it was still there and maybe I wanted a peek into a previous incarnation. The place was not busy and I sat near the stage pretending to drink a beer. The girls, although all undeniably beautiful, were terrible dancers or they didn't care. Every now and again one would try to engage me in conversation, inevitably they'd soon suggest we go up to the 'Executive lounge' and I'd decline each time.

One girl, however, a dark-skinned beauty, just chatted, didn't try to get me to go upstairs. She was surprisingly warm, even sweet, I liked her and I'll be sure to 'flesh' this story out later on, because there's more.

On the third day, my uncle Morris decided to visit. My dad and I went down to meet his taxi. As I lifted old Uncle Morris out of the car he handed me a dollar. I asked him what that was for and he said it was my tip, that I shouldn't expect any more because I wasn't a very good driver. When I finally made him understand that I was his nephew he demanded his dollar back.

Up in the apartment the old bugger kept looking over at me as though he couldn't understand why the taxi driver was still there. In fact, the only indication he knew me was when he turned to my dad and said: "What's with the beard?" After Morris' visit my folks had a fight and I went walking, again. Dinner was silent, terrible, and I was informed of an upcoming family wedding I was expected to join in, of a distant relation. All my relations were distant to me, very distant. But that's when I knew beyond any doubt that I had to get outta there, I had to get away.

I lurched through those first days, weeks, even months of my return to western life with some real trepidation coupled with some real hardships, but also with a real sense of purpose. I was very definite. It had been a great ride but I was done with ashram life, done with India. I wanted to see what might be beyond my stone hut and those high mountain peaks, to meet new people, maybe even start a family or join one already in progress. It seemed necessary, in order to continue my research into this world, reality, sexuality, (for sure sexuality,) old age, death, life. I was forty-eight at the time. I am much younger than that now.

Chapter 1

My Last Will and Testosterone

Advancing age is a well-charted voyage. Everyone knows what to expect, has heard all the platitudes. You'll still think of yourself as young, perplexed to see an old person in the mirror, surprised that you can't do things you used to be able to do and be disappointed by your failing memory. Everyone knows you'll start to repeat yourself and everyone knows you'll start to repeat yourself. Everyone knows you'll still think of yourself as young, that you'll be perplexed to see the old person in the mirror, surprised that you can't, well, you get the point. I recently sat down and wrote: 'My Last Will and Testosterone,' in order for me to slip peacefully into senility without the nagging feeling that I left the stove on.

last will and testosterone.

please be careful to execute these final instructions exactly and meticulously. that's very very important to me. just a minute: i'm presumably dead, so why should i care(?)

well, i'm writing these instructions now, which i actually couldn't care less about, simply because i'm able. it occurred to me in a rare moment of clarity that it'd be more difficult the closer i got to the end. maybe i'd forget what i wanted to say or, worse, maybe i'd say something i really didn't wanna say. certainly it wouldn't be the first time. and the last thing i'd need at that point is an old foot stuck in my mouth, especially my own. someone else's foot might be fun, but that's an entirely different matter. of course, also my hand might shake, eyes might fail. one thing is for sure: it would be impossible to write out any final instructions once deceased. as far as i know, nobody does that. i think it might even be illegal. so, although my life was hugely influenced by ram das' iconic phrase: 'be here now', sometimes it's appropriate to be here then, so to speak.

ok, so now i can't for the life of me remember what i wanted to say. oh yeah, ok, so of course i do hope you'll at least make sure i really am dead before disposing of the carcass. i saw a movie like that once and it wasn't pretty, but i digress. once you have definite confirmation of death, like maybe an official certificate of some sort, then the next thing is to make sure it's actually my body. no sense disposing of someone else's body. that'd be their problem and he or she, presumably a he, might have quite different ideas. i personally don't actually care if i'm cremated, buried or strapped to scaffolding as long as i am actually dead and it is actually my body. that's all i ask.

even now, as decrepit as i may be, it's hard to imagine myself dead. it always seemed as though that happened only to other people. in fact it has always happened only to other people. it has never once happened to me. i've always felt so alive, so vital, so terribly important. as a matter of fact i feel pretty good today.

it's virtually impossible for me to imagine that i've kicked the proverbial bucket and this letter is being read out. of course i never imagined i'd be wearing dentures either, not to mention incessantly asking people to repeat themselves or piddling in dribs and drabs for that matter. the point is i'm uncomfortable with this whole last will and patrimonial friggin inventory concept.

anyway, assuming i'm dead, you've got the right body and you're ready to move ahead, i lean toward cremation. it just seems the easiest, cheapest, cleanest way to finish off the whole sordid affair. but i'm flexible, or at least i used to be. do whatever the heck you wanna do. i really don't care. in the eventuality of cremation, however, i do care that you dump the ashes all in one place: either in the himalayan mountains or the gatineau hills, but all at once because i don't wanna feel too scattered. the easiest and simplest would be to dump the stuff out around here, maybe in the river when nobody's watching. whatever. come to think of it, i may not even be welcome back in india. i wrote a book called 'unprotected sects' that got me in trouble back there. it's on amazon, twenty bucks.

well, tears, sobs, general gnashing of teeth, while greatly appreciated, are honestly unnecessary. of course if you insist i won't stand in your way. presumably i'm unable to stand in your way. but nobody need feel too sorry for old nathan, howie, hansraj. i've done pretty well, had a good run. anything i've yet to learn will have to wait, whatever the heck that means. i do not require even a plaque on a bench. of course if you insist, the park overlooking the river, beside ernie's bench, might be nice.

but, really, just get on with it. the truth is i have no final instructions whatsoever. i just wanted to say goodbye, so long, namaste, best fishes, be well, live long, have fun, but don't do drugs. i love you guys and for heaven's sake be nice to each other.

ps: i'm really not into the whole scaffolding idea.

My urologist, Dr. Adamson, insisted I commit to a daily pill-swallowing routine. He insisted there would be no side-effects but I soon noticed that the label on the bottle warned, among other things, to consult a doctor should one get a painful erection that lasted more than four hours. I'm pretty darn sure I've never had an erection for four straight hours in my life, painful or otherwise. It'd probably take at least another four hours to see a doctor here in Québec anyway, during which time I would be sitting in the local emergency room with a throbbing boner while my neighbours, coughing and wheezing, tried not to look. Most prostate medicines have the opposite effect. I had been prescribed different pills for the same issue about a year and a half earlier in India. That stuff robbed me of my libido entirely and by the sixth or seventh month my penis seemed to have curled right up, resembling the dorsal fin of a captive dolphin.

My prostate seems to have become a 'large' problem. The first time I ever saw my new personal family physician, Dr. Lemieux, she announced matter-of-factly that she wanted to give me a digital rectal examination. I suggested we start with coffee, then maybe a movie, you know, take it slow. But she insisted. I don't know how it was for her but I found it rather disappointing. After it was over she told me to put my pants back on and left the room. I found it strange that she knocked before re-entering considering how intimate we had been only minutes earlier.

As I encounter the new and sometimes startling experiences of human aging myself, I keep thinking of the time I foolishly agreed to take my ninety-one-year-old dad on a cruise and how horribly he fretted over the possibility of having an 'accident' in the bed. I'd wake up to the sound of sobbing coming from the bathroom in the middle of every single night. I'd go in and coax him back to bed with assurances that I'd take care of any eventuality. You can bet there's more to this rather pissy story which I'm saving in order to describe fully and with a great flourish later on.

In the meantime, there was the wintry commuter flight from Ottawa to Toronto that illustrates the point just as wonderfully. I'd worked all day with no chance to eat or drink before running to catch my flight. I drank some water and a coffee there before realizing the six-seater plane had no bathroom. Unfortunately I was already on board and I had to pee. At the very same moment a lovely lady across the aisle attempted to engage me in conversation. I just couldn't. I was freaked, completely ignored her. I could not imagine holding 'it' for over an hour. It had become difficult to normally hold it for even a few minutes and being scared only made matters worse.

I knew the situation was hopeless. Still, I struggled for a while until I was in tremendous pain. What could I do? What could I do? With my coat wrapped around me I let 'er fly somewhere over Kingston. I could feel urine seeping down between my legs and into the seat but I was tremendously relieved. In fact I felt great. I was still piddling a bit as I leaned over and said to the lady across the aisle: "So are you from Ottawa or Toronto?"

Yogis allegedly age somewhat differently than the average human creature. Their deaths are called mahasamadhis, ultimate meditations. Sri Yukteswar (1836-1955) was the guru of Paramahansa Yogananda (1893-1952), one of the first to bring the science of meditation to the West. Sri Yukteswar had been a bramachari yogi his whole life, a formidable teacher and jnanavatar (said to have attained the level of 'incarnation of wisdom'). Right before his death he gathered his disciples, took his seat at the front of the hall and said: "You watch now. This is what it's all about." Then he proceeded to meditate, eventually slipping into mahasamadhi or death.

"Master's body remained unimaginably lifelike," wrote Yogananda in his book, 'Autobiography of a Yogi.' "He was sitting in lotus posture, a picture of health and loveliness. A short time before his death he had been ill. But the day of his ascension into the infinite, he had become completely well. No matter how often I looked at his form I could not realize that its life had departed. His skin was smooth and soft. In his face was a beatific expression of tranquility. He had consciously relinquished his body at the hour of mystic summoning."

While that example may remain a hard-to-imagine ideal, and while I'm afraid that my demise will almost certainly be far less dignified, I have personally witnessed some remarkable deaths. It is my observation that bramacharis, monks, and long-time meditators in general tend to 'die well.' For example, I visited my friend, Shankar, the day before he passed away. He had suffered a lot fighting a long battle with Prostate Cancer. When I asked how he was he smiled warmly. "Well, Hansraj," he said, "I'm fine, but this body is fucked." On another occasion I sat down beside Shakti Kumar, who was lying peacefully on his bed in a coma after a long battle with a brain tumor. I took his hand while his wife whispered, "Hansraj has come to say goodbye." He didn't say anything, of course, but he squeezed my hand lovingly. He died hardly a few minutes later.

The point is, being a bramachari yogi is in fact an investigation, a science, a life. This lifestyle can continue through the process of aging and dying; it is not just a series of postures, breathing exercises, or giving lip-service to the idea of meditation. It is the whole eight limbs of yoga (yam, niyam, asan, pranayam, pratyahar, dharana, dhyaan, samadhi). It's all of that. In fact it's all of life.

The human experiences of sex and of celibacy of course are counterparts, neither existing without the other. Avoidance of sex doesn't really come with a handbook. A generally sexless life will necessarily still allow for enough sexual encounters to last a lifetime. It may not make that life any less complicated but it may be the key to growing a spiritually transcendent experience. And presumably a spiritually transcendent experience opens one up to a greater understanding of life in its entirety.

Many self-proclaimed yogis in the West will be quick to point out that the word brahmacharya does not literally mean celibacy. They will tell you it means 'oneness with God' or 'behaviour that leads to realizing the Self.' That's quite true. Practically, however, it does mean celibacy. Or if it doesn't mean strict celibacy, a loose translation might at least be something like: 'recognition that the seminal fluids, that sticky gooey milky white-ish stuff that actually has the power of creation, should not be squandered stupidly.' There are no set rules of course. This is not the priesthood. This is an investigation into life and our bodies are our laboratories. Without rules, however, we really have only the experiences and opinions of past investigators, sages who have gone before us. We have a hope that their opinions are based on direct, personal experiences and that they're true. But we don't know that. We can't and shouldn't be certain. We each have to come to our own conclusions. That's what it means to be a bramachari yogi.

Having said that, it behooves us to at least listen to what they've written: that for real spiritual achievement, the yogi is well advised to keep his pecker in his pants, regardless of shrinkage. They may not have put it quite like that, of course, but I haven't always been a real good monk. I have, however, always been a real good bramachari. I do draw a distinction. Those sages talked about the need to retain the life-force and to look upon every woman as a mother, sister or daughter. They talked about the awakening of kundalini, the serpent power lying dormant within. They talked about realization of the infinite, the bliss of the absolute, samadhi and eventually mahasamadhi.

Chapter 2

Better Than Peanut Butter Cookies

It may of course never have occurred. The vision may have been the figment of a child's fertile imagination, an early hallucination. It may well have been just that. Perhaps it was wishful thinking. Certainly nobody needs to believe that it happened. However, I do have a memory sixty long years later of sitting alone in the garden outside my home. It wasn't a happy home, at all. I grew up with anger all around, yelling, uncomfortable silences. I preferred being alone, suffered some sadness, waited, wondered about things, had nasty headaches they called migraines. I was alone that day playing outside in the flower-bed when I saw (or imagined that I saw) the disembodied face of quite a happy, wise-looking old man with a flowing white beard. He smiled and I heard him say: "Don't worry. Just be patient. You will eventually find your true family." Did that happen actually and did I find my true family?

I was still pretty darn young at summer camp when I realized that rubbing my crotch around in the grass was surprisingly enjoyable, far better than peanut butter cookies. I became unusually focused and it just kept getting better and better. It may have been that same summer when I saw my first naked girl or perhaps the next. Whenever it was, the moment made a rather big impression on me. I was peeking through a hole in the wooden planks that faced the women's showers and, lo and behold, there was Angie in all her nubile glory. Angie. She was so beautiful. Her perky breasts jutting out while she lathered up her long straight hair with her back arched, unsuspecting. She was already a friend. After that, however, she became my constant day-dream, night-dream, wet-dream. I could not tear my eyes from her that afternoon and only stopped looking when a councillor grabbed me roughly by my shirt collar. But I swear he snuck a peek himself before dragging me away.

In the years that followed those days I continued my development into a screwed-up, pent-up adolescent. I was useless at relating to actual real live girls. I was nineteen when I lost my virginity, sort of. My two best friends and I drove across Canada and down to Mexico in an old Meteor that we had borrowed from one of their dads. The plan was that if we didn't get laid by the time we got to California, we would find a whore-house somewhere, anywhere. I, of course, totally blew the only real chance I had along the way. That was in Los Angeles and frankly I just froze, did not know what to do and eventually the girl just kinda gave up on me. The other two did better than I but still no banana, so to speak. Therefore we ended up driving to the 'Mustang Stud Ranch' outside of Reno, Nevada, one sultry summer afternoon.

We got out of the Meteor and walked to the gate on unsteady legs. Two German Shepherds lunged at us from inside their enclosure, slobbering and snarling. That did not improve my overall sense of terror. We recovered from the initial shock of the cadaverous-looking canine carnivorous creatures and rang the bell. The door was flung open by a large lady wearing a top-hat, a feather boa and little else. She greeted us warmly enough and instructed each to choose a girl from a line-up of lovelies.

I was the last to make a choice. Adrenaline had rushed to my head so that my eyes blurred. I went cross-eyed, couldn't focus. I went into some sort of catatonic state. Relating to women was beyond me. I would've been more comfortable yelling nonsense at them and then running off into some bushes. My two pals were no help. They'd already skipped happily away with their rented girlfriends.

The lady with the top-hat reminded me why I was there and what the procedure was. She had to repeat herself a couple of times. It's not as though I had to worry about being rejected. I simply went into some sort of altered state. Eventually I pointed, though not at any particular person. The madam asked me rather curtly to be a bit more specific. I couldn't speak. I just pointed again but in a slightly different direction. I heard snickering and, after a discussion I was not part of, they decided amongst themselves who I had chosen.

I was led to the lady's room. She took my ten bucks, helped undress me, stripped off the little she had on, flipped onto her back and in a totally business-like fashion instructed me to get on board. The soft body beneath me began to squirm and make primal noises. Of course, if she was having a good time it had little to do with me. I recall her drawling, "You gotta help too honey." Then she realized her suggestion was quite unnecessary. I was done, finished, kaput. So she simply rolled me off and went to clean up, I guess, and I was left to figure out whether that counted as my 'first time' or not.

I'm not sure what constitutes penetration, where the line is drawn, but I'm pretty darn sure I spilled the beans before passing through that gate. Of us three, I was the last to go in and the first to come out. I sat and waited for my friends in the front room of the joint. It was really some sort of huge mobile home with a few bedrooms, sofas, and a bar. I was mortified that I'd taken so much less time than my friends. They were both all smiles when they emerged. One was so energized by the experience that he insisted on driving all through the night. We had a great old time. We were three good friends who'd just had our first real sexual experience simultaneously. Of course I never mentioned my very real doubts.

About six months later I had dinner with one of those guys at his parents' home. It was a Toronto mansion, in fact, and though the parents didn't know it, I had been living in the basement all winter. We finished dinner and adjourned to the den to watch an episode of 'Sixty Minutes', which just so happened was featuring an exposé about brothels sprouting up all over the western United States. My buddy and I grinned at each other. When, however, the show began to feature a particularly popular cat-house called 'The Mustang Stud Ranch', our grins quickly faded. The rest was a bit of a blur but I remember two things: The first was hearing a lady tell the interviewer about a few young guys from Canada who'd driven down that summer in a big old Meteor and how they had been a nice change from the truckers they were used to. The second thing I remember was the sight of my buddy's dad peering over at his son, then me, then his son again with piercing knowing eyes. It had been after all his Meteor. But he never said a word.

I finished high school living in my 1963 Plymouth but shared a cheap apartment with a friend once I got to university. Woody Allen once wrote: "Sex is a lot like Bridge. If you don't have a good partner you'd better have a good hand." That was not a problem for me. I found myself with a different partner once or twice a week, a far cry from the inauspicious start of my sexual life or the bramachari I would later become. So many ladies, so little time. I once even found myself in bed with a she-male, which shocked the bejeesus outta me. I had it off with the maid of honor at my brother's wedding sometime between "I do" and the proverbial speeches, began to fall sick soon after that and ended up in hospital with Mononuclcosis.

That was a transformational experience for me. It was virtually the first time in my rather troubled, young life that I stopped. It was the first time I didn't feel I had to struggle. I didn't have to work two jobs while trying to get through a school year. I couldn't party. I couldn't screw, steal, stress, couldn't drink, do drugs or drive. I certainly couldn't smoke anything. I couldn't even wash or feed myself. I just stopped. I didn't consciously understand it at the time, and of course I had no ability to articulate it but that was effectively my first experience of meditation.

For the first time in my life I let go. I had no choice really which was good because who in their right mind does nothing? But during those days I experienced a sense of relaxation I had no idea was even possible. There was no hope for success or fear of failure. It was what it was, I was what I was. The people caring for me didn't know me, didn't care to know me. I was merely a living organism. It was an amazing cxpcricncc.

Unfortunately it faded fast once I got better. It quickly became a dim memory once I was well enough to make myself sick again. I really had no stomach for school by then so I flew to Jamaica where I developed a taste for Jamaican rum, Jamaican ganja and Jamaican women. Upon my return I took a low-paying joe-job with Canadian Press/Broadcast News on King Street and moved in with five guys in a terribly run-down, two-bedroom house in mid-town Toronto. That's where I met Elizabeth.

Elizabeth simply knocked on the door one evening as we sat around stoned, as usual, in front of the television. Apparently some folks I had hung out with in Jamaica, from Ann Arbour, Michigan, told her she really should look me up since she was going to Toronto on 'business.' She was, I soon learned, an exotic dancer. One of my house-mates, his blood-shot eyes as large as saucers at the sight of her, told me that my presence was required at the front door. She was so beautiful and I was so stoned that, although I invited her in, told her she could stay as long as she liked, I simply went back to my place on the couch.

Each guy who lived there and a couple who didn't tried in turn to 'get' with Elizabeth that first night. I was the only one who stayed away. That was my style and anyway I was too shit-faced to deal with it. Still, by the end of the evening I found her sitting beside me, slipping a couple of fingers in and out of my hand in a clear indication that she had made her choice and I was it. We went upstairs to what was to be our room for that night. It was really a tiny upper porch at the end of the hallway. Other than some carpeting the room was empty but we didn't care about that. We kissed, undressed each other, kissed again. I was ready for sex. What I wasn't ready for was love. I had no point of reference for that.

Elizabeth had one of the most perfect bodies I'd ever seen: classic full breasts, thin waist, long auburn hair, dark unreadable eyes. She was undeniably beautiful but it was her warm, welcoming, tender kiss that caught me off-guard and pulled me into a powerfully emotional sexual experience, the first ever.

She wrapped an arm around my neck while kissing me softly, slid her other hand down and stroked my already rigid cock. She was very much in charge, totally in control. She licked my chest, my stomach, swallowed my cock again and again until suddenly she lay down on the carpet on her back. She rubbed her hands up and down the inside of her thighs seductively as she spread her legs. As out of character as it may have been at the time, I went slowly at first. Each time I slid down into her I kissed her mouth. After a while, of course I began to lose my composure, plunging instead of sinking, quicker, harder. Our lips fused, she scratched my shoulders as our bodies slapped together in an ancient rhythm of life.

After, as we caught our breath side by side, Elizabeth kept kissing my face. She stroked my hair and nestled as close to me as possible. A few minutes later she got up and told me to stay where I was as she left the room. She returned with a warm wet towel and began to wash my body gently like I was her beloved or her child. Clearly she had plans for us. And so began the first real relationship of my young life.

Elizabeth was only a few years older than me unless we compared our mental ages, in which case she actually could've been my mother. She knew what she wanted: kids and a hobby farm. I'd obviously been pencilled in for that. She was the lady with a plan and I went with the flow. We moved into our own little apartment within a month and lived together for nearly two years.

About the time I shacked up with Elizabeth my career as a newsman with Canadian Press/Broadcast News was taking off. I had progressed from the office gofer to up-and-coming young jerk-on-the-go. The management shifted me through every department in order to give me a proper education. I learned all about the news business and about how incredibly skewered I could become should I stay the course. When the old hands were lying drunk under the desk I wrote their summaries for them. When management personnel staggered back from the press club I'd help them up the stairs. I listened to their troubles, dashed hopes and unfulfilled desires. I did all that was expected of me and was slated for big things: to move up the proverbial golden ladder, produce smart-ass kids, own a charming little hobby farm with my hot wife, become really miserable, get sick and die. It was all there in front of my eyes.

In the meantime Elizabeth and I were having fun making lots of money, drinking barrels of booze, smoking fields of dope, popping as many recreational drugs as a pharmacy could hold and fucking like crazy. I was heading exactly in the right direction, like most highly successful journalists before me. Life was an intoxicating blur punctuated by stagnant pockets of news-ink grey.

Elizabeth was not your garden variety stripper. Zana, as she was known professionally, was a gymnast, juggler, fire-eater, belly-dancer and ballerina. She would be as raunchy as you wanted her to be, and I wanted her to be quite raunchy quite often. She was the best damn stripper I'd ever seen and I worshipped her. Elizabeth was worldly, tough as nails and yet good-natured. We never argued, maybe because I just did whatever she wanted. There was a little Turkish restaurant nearby on Danforth Avenue where she would dance without being overly sensual when she wanted to stay close to home. Otherwise, for the big bucks she travelled.

When Elizabeth was on one of those 'business' trips I met up with an old high-school girlfriend, Vanna, who had always really liked me. We ended up back at my place. I expressed misgivings about what was obviously about to happen. Vanna insisted she didn't care that I actually lived with a lady and I got over my qualms as soon as she undressed and showed off her cute little body. She was petite in every way and looked so young without her clothes but it did feel strange fucking her on the same sofa Elizabeth and I made love on regularly.

Vanna's pubic hair was like steel wool. It hurt like hell when I entered her. As well, her vagina was like a clamp. It gripped me firmly and didn't seem to wanna let go. Needless to say I persevered. In spite of living with an exotic dancer I really didn't know much about satisfying a lady. I just knew how to fuck. And I did enjoy fucking Vanna, maybe because we just fit or because it was so wrong. Whatever might've been the case I clearly recall that in spite of my lack of carnal knowledge Vanna eventually became strangely quiet for a moment or two before all hell broke loose. Her whole body went into some sort of spasm as I continued to plunge into her. Her eyes rolled, legs began to shake uncontrollably, back arched. She moaned loudly even after I pulled out and came all over her stomach. I had never witnessed such an intense and dramatic orgasm.

Once Elizabeth returned from her trip I was mildly concerned that she'd realize I had been unfaithful. I wasn't concerned that she'd notice anything different about our sofa. Mostly I was worried she would wonder why my dick was so sore that I couldn't have sex with her for a few days. I was walking like a cowboy. I never did get together with Vanna again. I heard she tried to commit suicide sometime later and very nearly succeeded. That information really impacted me. Although there may have been no direct connection between the two events, that was when the strange, foreign, even alien concept of responsibility dawned upon me, perhaps for the first time.

Chapter 3

Mary Takes You Down

The beginning of the end of my relationship with Elizabeth, and the end of the beginning of everything yet to come, was when we met Eric. He was a short, wizened old fellow with a straggly grey beard and a gravelly laugh. Eric had been a friend of Richard Alpert, Timothy Leary, Ken Kesey and other pioneers of the so-called New Age. However, by the time he hid at our place in Toronto for a while he had sworn off hard drugs and had instead embraced meditation. It was the first time I heard the word and it caught my attention. The possibility that a person could directly experience one's source, one's originality, where one comes from, where one goes, while still living actually did more than catch my attention. It grabbed me like an undertow, threw me around and swept me away. I concluded that if what the ancient sages had said was true, as Eric had described, then why not me? I was not at all certain of any of it but I sure wanted to find out. I also had a dim memory of the time I lay in a hospital room, helpless, completely dependent and totally relaxed.

The result of coming in contact with Eric and that information, that life-altering possibility, precipitated several changes rather swiftly. Eric used to make rather beautiful pointillist landscape drawings in ink, one dot at a time. And he always wrote 'the world is a dot and each dot a world.' I have no idea what ever became of those drawings created with such patience. I've no idea what became of Eric. As a matter of fact I've no idea what became of Elizabeth. i've never even been able to recall her last name.

My work was easy. I could write my summaries within a half hour, leaving a half hour free before the next, plenty of time to go out onto the fire-escape and smoke a joint. One late Friday night, when no lady editors were ever scheduled to work, I intelligently decided to smoke a big fat spliff while sitting comfortably in the ladies' lounge. Predictably, that was the one night there was in fact a lady working late. The room thick with smoke, my feet up, tie loosened, shirt un-tucked and in she walked. She screamed as though I had attacked her and went running through the news-room. It just did not look good. Subsequently, after a few days, much arguing, many meetings and plenty of whispered gossiping, it was decided that I would not be fired.

Presumably management realized how incredibly unfair that would have seemed since I was the one who most often helped them up the stairs when they were too plastered to make it on their own. In the end it was decided I would be demoted to the regional desk, which was worse than being fired. It was incredibly boring. On the upside, it gave me even more free time. So in addition to smoking dope out on the fire-escape I utilized my new-found extra time to learn about a sensitive little operation called the Voice Room. In that room, where sound-bites and audio news clips were gathered, only one guy was allowed and it sure wasn't me. However, the fellow in question was a brute of a man, Mr. Hugh Scanlin, a Vietnam vet prone to inappropriate outbursts, had somehow become a friend of mine. He began to let me in secretly and show me how it all worked. Eventually I got pretty good at his job. He soon let me take over for a few minutes each day.

On one such occasion, while Hugh was out grabbing a burger, a remarkable thing happened. I got a call from a radio station in Kenora, Ontario, where an aboriginal fellow had just tried to rob the local bank. The robbery had gone badly. I really don't remember why. But I recall that, with a small bomb strapped against his chest, he took the bank manager hostage. He was surrounded by the totality of the Kenora police force, quite a few RCMP officers and many on-lookers outside the bank, on the street, even on roof-tops. And it just so happened that the newsroom was on the second floor of a building right across from the scene. It was a big scoop for us, something that rarely ever happened. The story was of national interest, I believe, due to the aboriginal component.

While Hugh munched blissfully on his burger somewhere, a major drama was unfolding inside the voice room. The big boys from upstairs had crowded into the small space and were horrified to find me manning the controls. But they knew nothing about working that room. I was the only one capable and frankly I was enjoying it thoroughly. I kept the caller describing the scene and offering background information while I filtered the reports and sent them across the country to every radio station that subscribed to Canadian Press/Broadcast News. Conscious of the hundreds of thousands of dollars I was indirectly bringing in to the coffers, I worked the room with a flourish. I was on display like a concert pianist at Carnegie Hall, in the zone like a basketball player at Madison Square Garden. And boy was I stoned.

The standoff dragged on and the newsman in Kenora was running out of things to say but I insisted he stay on the line. In fact I asked if there was a phone-booth near the action on the street. He said there was. Now it just so happened that I had very recently learned how to undo the receiver of a phone and attach alligator clips from a tape recorder to make it act as a microphone. Hugh had taught me how. I told the guy in Kenora what to do as though I was an expert and insisted he immediately send someone down. The big boys, who were all actually big, appeared to be thoroughly non-plussed. Hugh returned but was immediately told that his services were no longer required. I was aware of that but being in full stride I was not to be distracted.

Meanwhile, just as an unsuspecting, aspiring Kenora cub reporter set up the tape recorder in the phone booth all hell broke loose. The robber walked out of the bank behind the manager. Seeing an officer raise his rifle the guy reached for his gun, a few shots rang out and there was an explosion. The bomb had detonated obliterating the poor bastard, seriously injuring the manager and knocking many people on their asses. The tempered glass of the phone booth shattered cutting the reporter badly but, hell, we caught it all on tape.

I can still see the look of absolute glee the head honchos wore as they congratulated each other, making no attempt to hide their feelings. They congratulated me too, clapped me on the back and shook my hand. Hardly a month after being demoted I was promoted. I was offered exclusive control of the Voice Room which I accepted only after they agreed to hire Hugh back as my partner. I quit about a month after that.

My quitting came as a great shock to everyone. It infuriated my employers and Elizabeth was equally unimpressed. Soon after that, I also quit smoking, became a vegetarian, stopped gobbling drugs and guzzling booze. It was horrible. Meditation was ruining my life and I had hardly just begun.

Elizabeth had already banned Eric from staying with us and she disapproved of the change in my attitude, my diet, my choice of reading material. I certainly wasn't as much fun as I'd been and I suppose I looked less and less like husband or father material. Since I no longer had work she insisted I travel with her as a kind of road manager. We went to a seedy, gothic place called The Black Box in Halifax which was where I decided to return home rather than carry on to The Lobster Trap in Amherst. The thing is, I was weary. I was all fucked out. I had very little left or so it seemed to me even before I ever heard about continence or moderation, the power of celibacy or the science of brahmacharya. We said goodbye and I helped her onto her specially-ordered mini-bus. I left for the airport and that was the last time I ever saw Elizabeth. She never returned, just kept on going I guess.

Master of my own domain once again, like it or not, I certainly had time to focus on the meditative way of life Eric had described. Spiritual books and scriptures of all sorts took his place as my teacher and soon my domain became a pathetic little shack out west. During the winters I would write unimportant articles for unimportant papers on the gulf islands and in the summers I'd go tree-planting in the north-country.

Later on I travelled southward and moved to a deserted beach in Mexico, became a fruitarian and experienced my first attempt at remaining strictly celibate. I continued reading a lot, classics such as 'Be Here Now', 'Autobiography of a Yogi', 'Cutting Through Spiritual Materialism', 'The Tibetan Book of the Dead', 'The Aquarian Gospel of Jesus the Christ' and many more. Quitting cigarettes along with cocaine and several other recreational drugs did not faze me. It became a question of whether I intended to be in charge of my own mind, not that I even really understood what that meant at the time. It took a while longer to quit smoking dope. My head filled with stories of Himalayan yogis, the experiences and remarkable romantic lives of ancient enlightened saints.

I came up for air one sultry night in 'Barra de Navidad' and noticed an especially attractive woman drinking a beer in a café. I had been in Mexico for several months mostly living on a deserted beach about five kilometres from the village past a coconut grove. Her name was Mary and she'd been in a bad car accident a year earlier, had a terrible limp, was down south to continue her recovery. Old habits die slowly so I struck up a conversation and by the end of the evening Mary insisted on joining me at the beach for a couple of days. This was both great and terrible because of course I really wanted her and I really did not want her. I was screwed without even touching her.

At the time, two other guys were camping out on that beach and like me they believed themselves to be great brahmacharis, having sworn off all sexual contact with the female species. Mary however was not really buying what we were selling. What she had expected to happen between the two of us did not happen, although she will never know the things we did together within my imagination. With efficiency she turned her attention to one of my beach-mates, a self-proclaimed enlightened guru of the New Age. He was forever lecturing his friend who I presumed was some sort of disciple.

I vividly recall that night I noticed him lecturing Mary on the virtues of abstinence. They were standing together near the ocean's edge in the moonlight when I realized that while he pontificated Mary was simultaneously actually jacking him off. I was sincerely and utterly disgusted. I could see her hand sliding up and down in the shadows as he continued to rant on about the virtues of celibacy. After a while I heard his voice rise a little until he made a sound like a startled pig. Immediately thereafter the class apparently was over. He skipped off into the ocean and she headed back to where she kept her towel. That upset me terribly because it was so incredibly hypocritical of him and, well, maybe because it wasn't me.

During those months in Mexico, aside from meditating, reading, swimming and climbing, I decided I really should prepare my carcass for so-called spiritual advancement. I became a devotee of a doctor who had cured himself of Bright's disease using a diet he'd devised. He called it 'Dr. Arnold Ehret's Mucous-less Diet Healing System.' Basically one starves the body during long fasts interspersed with what he termed a paradisiacal diet. I'd fast for up to a week at a time drinking only coconut juice followed by a few weeks of eating citrus fruit in the morning, sweet fruit at mid-day, then raw cabbage in the afternoon. Walking behind me might've been unpleasant but I could shimmy up coconut trees like nobody's business. After surviving a disease that should've killed him, however, Dr. Ehret slipped on a slick bit of pavement in new shoes, fell backward and conked his head on a curb. Apparently he died instantly and, I might add, the irony was not lost on me.

Mary came back to see me once about a week later when I was quite alone on my beach but I could not deal with her. By then I could barely relate to anyone. I rarely went into town. I could talk to the falcons that nested high up on the cliffs. I could swim with the fish that stopped scattering as I entered their water. But I continued to have trouble relating to humans, women, and I could not talk to Mary. It was very uncomfortable and she left within an hour or two.

The question at this point of the story begs asking: what the fuck? I mean to say, what the fuck? I mean, what the fuck is this supposed need to practice celibacy for the spiritual aspirant?

A possible answer constitutes a large part of the more esoteric teachings of the science of yoga, an aspect of the science as previously pointed out rarely discussed, little known, somewhat controversial, often ridiculed, refused, refuted and reviled. And it has ruled my life. For me, understanding the theory came long after a kind of blind faith in the practice. I don't even honestly recall where I first heard about the concept of brahmacharya as I originally understood it. It just intuitively seemed to be a formula for greatness. It just instantly made sense to me and fortunately or unfortunately it still does, albeit in its less fundamental form.

Chapter 4

Publicly Endorsed Masturbation

Baba Hari Das once wrote to me on his blackboard: 'I never knew a householder that didn't have problems and I never knew a monk that didn't have problems'. The esoteric teachings of the yogic life are either little known or studiously ignored by virtually all western hatha yogis and meditators, even now. Whenever it may have been that I read about the secret science of brahmacharya with its inherent hardships and rewards, the information struck me deeply and I've been affected by it ever since. The theory is simple, the practice not so simple.

The ancient sages have said that each of us possess a store-house of energy at the base of the spine. That energy, that life force, is expelled constantly through the senses. A bramachari attempts to redirect that energy for the sake of optimizing health, personal power and for spiritual awakening. He or she decides to change the die that was cast at the moment of birth. A bramachari takes a vow of celibacy or at least sexual continence and institutes a practice of dhyaan, meditation, consciously guarding the balance between extroversion and introversion.

As I've said, many will point out that the literal meaning of the term is not celibacy but rather oneness with God, whatever the heck that means. Nobody wants to accept a need for celibacy, continence or even moderation. Hell, although drastically more relaxed now I'll probably be eighty-five, dying of some withering disease while still undressing the nurses with my eyes. The harsh reality is that the practice of bramacharya is an integral part of any dedicated quest for self-realization. I know this from personal experience. Without meditation, however, celibacy can lead men to the buggering of choir boys, furry farm animals or other weird shit. It can drive you nuts, especially when you're young. With meditation you've got a fighting chance, just a fighting chance. Ultimately, however, celibacy can lead to all that good stuff flooding one's system. Just as ice becomes water and water becomes vapor, semen eventually turns into a more subtle substance called 'ojas', 'tejas' and then 'bindu'. As a meditator, this increasingly more subtle and powerful energy moves on up through opened channels supplying one with health, intelligence, real bliss and true knowledge.

Women did not have access to the education their male counterparts were getting. K.A. Kunjakkan wrote in her book 'Feminism and Indian Realities', "Women are not expected to undergo 'Sannyasa ashrama' also because of its hard and definite ordeals of sufferings and sacrifices. Can the feminists feel there is discrimination against women here?" She elaborates on the way women have historically been separated from spiritual practice and learning. "One of the chief duties of the women was to bear children and to rear them up. In view of spiritual practice, women were exempted from duties concerning moral purification or spiritual advancement. It was believed that a woman attained purification and reached the goal by associating herself with her husband in the religious exercises, in the worship through sacrifices and vows etc."

There are of course many esteemed and honoured female yogis, though it may not be easy to track down bramacharinis. Regardless of their sexual practices a handful of women are honored in traditional spiritual texts. In the Brahadaranyaka Upanishad we are told about the learned lady Gargi Vacaknavi who held discussions with Yajnavalkya and nonplussed him with her searching questions. Another scholar Maitreyi, wife of Yajnavalkya, also participated in the learned discourses.

I have no real idea of how it all works for the ladies, the nuns, yoginis, bukkhinis and bramacharinis among us. After a lifetime of self-observation and experimentation I can really only speak for the guys. Perhaps I can only speak for myself.

Dr. Charmaine Saunders, guru in her own right and expert columnist to 'Women's Health and Fitness' magazine,' says the following about male and female experiences of celibacy: "Men will often use sex as a cure-all for quarrels and arguments whereas women will be turned off by those same things and either withdraw or reject advances. Women have an interesting cut-off mechanism which amounts to withdrawal, both sexually and emotionally. As female sexuality is more internal and contained it's a lot more possible to shut down physically. Sexual desire is then sublimated into other activities/interests"

Perhaps, then, greater emphasis exists on the importance of male celibacy not only because of a patriarchal dominance throughout history but also because, well, men need more help with self-control. Women allegedly have a powerful built-in 'cold shower' mechanism. Still it seems to depend on the woman. Those who choose celibacy for religious or moral purposes may still experience an overspill of sexual energy into the physical form: the female wet dream. It's apparently more common than we think. "I remember a radio caller telling me she kept waking up with spontaneous orgasms because she didn't believe in casual sex or masturbation. I had to explain to her that her body was naturally releasing sexual tension," recalls Dr. Saunders.

In the nineteenth century Alice Bunker Stockham was the fifth female doctor in the United States. She was also quite interested in the secrets of tantra and the control of the orgasm response. She even travelled to northern India in search of answers. I don't know if it was fun, enlightening, how far Alice went down that rabbit hole but she subsequently publicly endorsed masturbation for both men and women. She promoted orgasmic control only as a form of pregnancy prevention, to help fix failing marriages or, somehow, for women to gain social and political equality. She was less interested in spiritual matters. In her book, 'Tokology', Stockham wrote: "A method adopted by the Oneida community (those who practice continence), is used with complete satisfaction by many married people. In this the sexual relation is entered upon but not carried to completion. Some call it 'secular absorption.' No discharge is allowed. People practicing this method claim the highest possible enjoyment, no loss of vitality and perfect control of the fecundating power."

In her paper, 'Sacred Sex,' American freelance writer Catherine Yronwode wrote: "It has been my personal experience that traditional Hindu tantric teachers tend to emphasize the conservation and elevation or self re-absorption of male seed (semen, prostatic fluid or bindu) as an important method of tantra yoga that will lead the disciple to liberation from future rebirths. And there is apparently no place in that scheme for the female except as a hand-maiden to the male aspirant."

Swami Shivananda claimed that a sage will see "the one underlying eternal immortal Self in a female and a male. He will not have any difference of feeling when he touches a book, a log of wood, a piece of stone and the body of a female. There is no idea of sex in a 'Jnani'. Such must be the condition of mind of a man who is established in Brahmacharya". Of course it might be rather difficult for the bramachari-in-training to see the immortal non-dual self in a woman when he is encouraged, as part of his training, to also look upon women as crafty seductresses. "Though females are more passionate, yet they have more power of restraint than males. After enticing men, they keep quiet...When once man falls into the trap or net spread out by woman, there is no escape for him"

Where men are considered more intellectually powerful than women the resource is tainted. While Swami Shivananda gives plenty of great advice as well as legitimate warnings, modern women may well not relate to every aspect of his teachings. Who could blame them? Dr. Saunders believes that female celibacy is a viable option that doesn't necessarily have to be affected by male behaviour. Instead, she sees it as a viable lifestyle that requires tools and practices to maintain balance, like so many other aspects of life. "Is celibacy a hardship? Only if it's not chosen. As a way of life, it need not be a burden if sexual tensions are released in some other healthy way".

I must add here that, while my adult life has been ruled by the practice of brahmacharya, I do find the extremism and rigidity of Swami Shivananda, Mahatma Gandhi and others, somewhat discomforting.

"Women who are chaste can be called as bramacharinis," Shivananda wrote. "Through the force of brahmacharya only, many women of yore have done miraculous deeds and shown to the world the power of chastity...such is the glory of womanhood. Such is the power of chastity or brahmacharya." He immediately returns to focusing on the liberation of men after this patronizing passage leaving women very little to work with. What Shivananda does convey is that he leaves no doubt about his belief in the science, its rewards and also its difficulties. "It is easy to tame a wild tiger or an elephant. It is easy to play with the cobra. It is easy to walk over the fire. It is easy to get victory in the battlefield. But it is difficult to eradicate lust."

He goes on to recommend regular meditation, a pure vegetarian diet, good company, and the study of scriptures. That's pretty reasonable in my semi-humble opinion. But he also suggests a few more questionable practices, like living in seclusion for many months or even years beside any holy river, envisioning women with their skin peeled away, cold baths every morning at 4 a.m., the constant wearing of tight latex loin-cloths, things like that. Ok, I made up the latex part but what is a holy river anyway?

Sexual abstinence has found an interesting niche in the West: sports figures have exhibited an awareness of the importance of conserving one's energy by abstaining from sexual activity before events. Apparently Rocky Marciano would stay away from his wife sexually for months before a major bout. I wonder how that marriage worked out. Muhammad Ali too was said to abstain for at least six weeks prior to a fight. Suzanne Dando, a British Olympic gymnast, said she stayed away from sex during her whole career. Apparently she was afraid of getting knocked up. On the other hand, the only time the great Bob Beamon ever had sex before a long-jump competition, according to him, was on the eve of his world-record-shattering jump at the 1968 Mexico City Olympics. His record stood for 23 years.

In 'The Multi-Orgasmic Man', Mantak Chia and Douglas Abrams wrote the following: "The image of the unsatisfied woman whose lover ejaculates, grunts, and collapses on top of her is so common that it has become a cultural joke. But, the exhaustion that men feel after ejaculating is as old as the first coital groan. Peng-tze, a sex advisor to the famed Yellow Emperor, reported almost five-thousand years ago, '...after ejaculating, a man is tired, his ears buzz, his eyes are heavy and he longs for sleep. He is thirsty and his limbs feel weak and stiff. In ejaculating he enjoys a brief moment of sensation but then suffers long hours of exhaustion.'"

In the same book the authors talk about Taoists, a group of 'seekers' in ancient China around 500 B.C.E., who were extremely interested in health and spirituality. In 'The Discourses on the Highest Tao Under Heaven' it is written: "If a man has intercourse without spilling his seed his vital essence is strengthened. If he does this twice his hearing and vision are made clear. If three times his physical illnesses will disappear. The fourth time he will begin to feel inner peace. The fifth time his blood will circulate powerfully. The sixth time his genitals will gain new prowess. By the seventh his thighs and buttocks will become firm. The eighth time his body will radiate good health. The ninth time his life span will increase." Wow. I mean, wow!

Chia and Abrams point out that, while the Taoist's description may be an exaggeration, the importance of conserving one's semen has long been upheld. In many species, once the seed has been given the body of the animal begins to deteriorate. "Salmon, for example, die soon after they spawn. Anyone who has spent time gardening knows that plants die or go dormant once they have given their seed. Plants that are prevented from going to seed live longer than those that are not" Sure, humans don't work exactly like salmon or dill, although I do know a few who are close to it. Still, there's something to be said for patterns in nature. Nature doesn't screw around even though we do.

By not falling over the threshold in the ascent to orgasm, men apparently can produce more sperm than ever. That being said, I'm not sure how much hard data has been legitimately derived from our grandfathers' emissions. According to the research of Danish endocrinologist Niels Skakkebaek, the sperm counts of men in the United States and twenty other countries have fallen dramatically over the last half-century–by as much as fifty percent. The cause of this precipitous decline is still being debated and possible culprits range from tight underwear to chemical pollutants.

University of Florida researcher Louis Guillette told a panel of U.S. congressmen: "Every man in this room is half the man his grandfather was....if you have low sperm-count you will be relieved to know there are sexual exercises you can use to help raise it. However, engaging in non-ejaculatory sex is the most important thing you can do to increase the volume, concentration and count of your sperm. According to Western medical research each day you do not ejaculate you increase your sperm count by fifty to ninety million sperm."

One of the pieces of information I came across upon my return from India, which really shocked and amazed me, concerned the penis size of snapping turtles. It seems that the reproductive organs of the Lake Ontario Snapping Turtles have become approximately fifteen percent shorter than what they ought to be. That must really get them snapping.

Apparently some University of Guelph zoologists spent years studying the shriveling penises of the turtles. And while one has to wonder what the zoologists' own home life must be like, what motivates them to delve into such research, what drives them on, in fact, one has to applaud their diligence not to speak of their passion for detail. Turtle eggs that were collected produced also turtles with other deformities or never hatched at all, a far preferable alternative from my point of view. According to the same article on March 7th, 1999, in the Ottawa Citizen, the salmon in Lake Erie are also losing their male traits, the heavy jaw and red, cherubic colour, for the same or similar reasons. The article also pointed out that young Florida alligators subjected to a pesticide spill had very small penises and abnormal testicles. As well, Herring Gulls on the Great Lakes are being called now by the dubious handle of Gay Gulls.

The point of all this is that recent findings apparently show men in Europe and North America mirror these findings in wildlife. And while the women of the species, if now given the chance to take over, may finally get it right, it does bother me and I haven't even brought up yet the case of the Mudpuppies in the St. Lawrence, the Ottawa River and the Great Lakes. They're turning up with extra, missing or fused toes, missing or misshapen legs.

As well, again, one wonders how that all actually works in a woman's body? Does sexual abstinence result in more plentiful fertile eggs? Obviously males and females, while often on the same bed, have never really been on the same page about sex and this discussion is no exception. Had Swami Shivananda found the girl of his dreams or been born in the twenty-first century, would he have seen things differently? One thing is for sure: his sperm count must've been off the charts!

Chapter 5

Inappropriate Advances

O nce Mary limped away I really had to face the fact that I remained just as screwed up as ever. That didn't seem right. As well, after months of telepathically asking those falcons to come down and sit beside me, one actually did. It happened so naturally that for a moment or two I didn't even react. That incident, in addition to the sighting of a great white shark near the rocks where I swam most days, seemed like a sign from above and below that it was time to move on.

In Puerto Vallarta I met quite a few folks who were disciples of Baba Free John from San Francisco, which was where I wanted to go. A gay couple befriended me and offered a spot in their yellow Volkswagen bug, only they had to wait a few days because one of them had Montezuma's Revenge. Meanwhile, the healthy one made no secret of the fact that he liked me. I mean he liked liked me. While I appreciated the compliment and their particular slant on the philosophy of oneness and love, I didn't know if I could put that into practice. Still I did need a ride, he was kind of cute and I had recently disappointed someone horribly.

Well, anyway, the sick one used my room that night and I stupidly ended up in bed with the other. We slipped between the sheets. The moon was full, flooding the room with a soft glow as tree shadows danced upon the walls. It was warm. There was no breeze. We only wore our briefs into bed which we soon took off and turned to face each other. It was a romantic moment. As soon as he reached out and stroked my chest, however, I totally understood the phrase 'my skin crawled'. Of course he felt my revulsion and I apologized profusely but there was no way that 'it' was gonna happen. He was quiet for a few moments. I actually thought he was going to cry. Instead he asked if I would hold his hand. I took his hand. I lay there holding it wondering how long I'd have to stay like that when I realized he was jerking off.

Two days later I got Montezuma's Revenge. After living on a beach for a year and a half without ever having a sick day I had my head in a bucket and my ass on a toilet, within a week of being in the city. That went on for a couple of more days. I thought I was better when my friends were ready to head north but I was quite mistaken. I had to ask them to stop again and again all along the Mojave Desert. Eventually they got fed up with pulling over and insisted I ingest some pills that they said would cork me up. That worked like a charm only my ankles swelled up like elephant's feet.

Not long afterward, their car's engine blew. Smoke billowed out from under the hood as we ground to a halt. The guys had apparently neglected to check the oil for a long long time. I bailed out and began hitch-hiking, secretly happy to be rid of them. It was like being on a vacation with my aunts Doris and Phyllis, together, something I would never do. Sometimes it's just better to be all alone in the middle of a desert. Eventually I got picked up by a drug enforcement, D.E.A., agent. Needless to say I was full of praise for the good work his people were doing in the war on drugs. I was on my best behavior all the way to Tucson. It was the easiest border crossing I'd ever experienced.

In Tucson Mr. Agent Man invited me to be his guest for dinner at the Ramada Inn. I didn't want to seem ungrateful so I proceeded to do something pretty foolish: after two years of strict vegetarianism, fruitarian-ism and some serious Ghandi-esque fasting, I ate a big chicken dinner. After all, it was free. Even before finishing, however, it was obvious a volcano was about to erupt in my pants. I had to run in a panic to the bathroom straight through a whole herd of Shriners. Once inside, the situation quickly deteriorated. It went from bad to worse as I shuffled from stall to stall. When one wouldn't flush anymore I'd move on to the next. I was effectively uncorked.

While sitting in the last stall huffing and puffing from sheer exhaustion, I glimpsed some of the Shriners piling in, talking, laughing and falling over each other. Through the space between the door and the wall I saw their tasseled red hats sitting precariously upon their drunken heads. Then I heard one say, "So, Georgy boy howz the little lady? Jeezus H. Christ, what's the smell!? Back off! Back off! Everybody get the hell outta here!" I do believe the Ramada Inn in Tucson, Arizona, had to renovate after my visit. My ankles, however, shrank right back to their normal size.

The bay area had always been good to me. Hitching from there to the east, not so good. On that occasion I had a vague plan to visit Chogyam Trungpa in Boulder, Colorado, but I got stuck on the salt flats in the mid-west for several days. It felt like how I imagined it'd be on the moon had I managed to land just as the craft disintegrated and there was no hope in hell of ever getting off. It's not that people didn't stop. Oh, they stopped alright. And then they'd take right off again the moment I got close enough to reach for the door, a cloud of dust covering me, hoots and howls filling my ears. When I did finally get a friggin' lift the man, dressed in black, was going all the way to Chicago. After languishing for so long on the salt flats I decided to go all the way. It made no difference to me at all that he was driving a hearse with a coffin in the back, that there may have been a dead body in there. I was comfortable and I was moving. That's how I ended up bypassing Boulder and visiting my old summer camp buddy Danny in Windsor.

Danny's little sister Seyna had only just returned from a Vippassana meditation retreat. This fascinated the heck outta me. I wanted to know all about it and if there might be any upcoming retreat scheduled that I could join. Seyna made a couple of calls and learned about one starting soon outside of Berkeley, at a Jesuit retreat centre in the Sierra Nevada Mountains. There were a couple of snags, though. Firstly, it was a thirty-one day retreat strictly for veteran students. Normally Vippassana retreats were ten days long. Longer retreats were considered too intense, even dangerous for new meditators. Secondly, it had just taken me over ten days to get to Detroit/ Windsor from San Francisco. Nevertheless, I was so determined or so annoying that the folks there agreed to include me... if I made it to their place in Berkeley before they left for the retreat. That only gave me three days.

Danny and Seyna drove me to Detroit and left me against their better judgment on the side of the interstate. Something immediate and amazing happened to me then, something so unusual that I remember it still with a sense of wonder. I was whisked across the country by a series of transport trucks even though it was contrary to both their union regulations and the law. Every time one had to let me go the driver would use a secret code on the CB radio to arrange for another to pick me up. I'd be instructed to wait at a truck stop for a rig with running shoes dangling from its back doors or a bra strapped to its antenna and jump in the cab when the driver went in the diner for coffee. Basically I was on the move day and night. It had taken me so long to get from the west coast to Detroit but it hardly took me three days to return. The Vippassana people in Berkeley were surprised to see me and had no choice but to include me in the retreat.

The term Vippassana means insight into the true nature of reality. For me it was an insight into the true nature of my fucked-upness. As a Vippassana retreat is for many first-timers, it was hellish. Only this one was three times as long. One is left alone in silence with no reading, writing or hard drugs of any sort. I could always sit and I guess I looked alright. It was just really fortunate that no one could see my thought-bubbles. Still, it did have its moments.

After the discourse on the third evening, as I lay down in the darkness of my little sleep-cubicle with my eyes closed, I began to see a bright sun with doves flying into it from below and then out the top again and again, over and over. Eventually I got up and turned the light on. As I lay back down I continued to see the vision. It didn't matter whether the light was on or not. That went on for most of the night and in the morning I was able to mention the experience to the teacher, the erstwhile Mr. Robert Hover. All he said was that I was well-suited to 'the work'. I was quite high and happy after that, for a while. Mostly it was a living hell.

Finally finally the last day arrived. It might've arrived sooner for me had anyone left a shotgun hanging about but I made it all the way to the thirty-first day. I didn't crap in my pants or make any inappropriate advances to the girls. I didn't bark profanities in the middle of long sessions. I didn't even consider Mr. Hover the anti-Christ, although the thought had crossed my mind more than once. I had all those things going on in my mind as I seemed to be peacefully observing the transitory nature of all forms and phenomena.

The only other first-timer there was an elderly Jesuit priest. He was allowed to join because it was his retreat centre, which made sense. Well, on the way out of the hall, after the vow of silence was lifted, that old guy quickly shuffled up to my side and wanted to chat. Unfortunately, chatting was the very last thing I wanted to do. He grabbed my arm and said, "I was watching you a lot. You're an incredible meditator. You can sit for hours." I nodded my head in a sage-like and humble manner, but he continued. "You know," he said, "I now remember why I originally wanted to become a minister and watching you really inspired me." I nodded again while trying to move away. I really was in no condition to talk. I was totally shattered and just wanted to hide.

"Tell me please," he continued, holding my arm, "what was it like for you?" He had no idea what he was dealing with but he insisted: "What was the experience like for you? I am very interested." Obviously I had to say something. I opened my mouth. I tried to squeak out a good word or two. Unfortunately the sounds that came out were not good, not pretty, not even real words. "Argh! argh! argh!" I must've looked like I was choking on a piece of tofu. My face went beet red, my eyes were popping. That old Jesuit minister spun 'round, threaded his way through the crowd and out the door faster than he'd probably moved in years, and that was the end of my first real meditation retreat.

For the next few years I basically travelled from retreat to retreat, sitting with Robert Hover and Ruth Dennison. My migraines ended forever during a retreat at a mountain-top farm outside of Eugene, Oregon. A real doozy flared up about the third day in and somehow Ruth tuned into it, came up to me as we walked meditatively in-between sittings, and asked what was happening. After I told her I suffered from migraines she simply suggested I watch it. I clearly recall thinking, 'that's your great advice?' She turned right back to me and said I should stop owning it. "It's pain, not your pain. Follow the strands of it to their source. Watch with equanimity." I would have preferred drugs, of course, but I had very little choice but to follow her instructions.

As we sat during that very next hour I watched the pain. I observed the pain. I followed the strands, practiced equanimity. For most of that session my point of attention was clear and obvious until all of a sudden the headache burst, spreading an amazing, soothing, tingling heat throughout my entire body. It was a truly incredible body-rush and I began to rock back and forth in a kind of rapture. Yet the most remarkable aspect of the situation for me was the realization that the pleasure was essentially, in a way, the same as the pain. It dawned upon me that I had to be as detached from the pleasure as from the pain. It too would not last.

I continued to practice a rather strict, stoic form of meditation by the time, during a subsequent retreat, I took on a vow to sit for four hours in full-lotus position. So I meditated and I meditated. And when the gong sounded to signify the beginning of the final hour, I hoped for deep insight and wonderful progress, because I was in excruciating pain. It was not my pain. It was just pain. It felt like my pain. It was hard to believe it wasn't my pain. But I apparently was not supposed to own it. Still it seemed to be growing stronger. I recalled the migraine I'd sat through not so many weeks earlier. Meanwhile, I began to feel like Wily Coyote from the old Road Runner cartoons, trying to put on the brakes before falling over the edge of a cliff, helplessly watching the edge zoom inexorably closer, digging his heels in to no avail.

At that moment I made a conscious decision to continue. Aside from being pretty well locked into position and having taken the four-hour vow, I wanted to know. I really wanted to know what lay beyond the edge, to jump off into the unknown. The pain and the heat in my legs and back had built up like a pressure-cooker. However, when the pressure finally released it was not dramatic. It was not a body rush. It was more like a time-lapse video of a flower opening. Consciousness was transported out of the confines of the body.

My direct perception was that whoever remained in that hall transcended with me, all of us together; one consciousness, one life. A vehicle drove up and we could see it. Without leaving the hall we could see he had a long ladder on the side of his van. We could see the man himself get out and go to the door. And when he got no response from knocking and noticed all the shoes, we saw his expression of panic. He stumbled back to his van and drove quickly away. I felt like laughing but didn't dare.

My body cooled and I re-entered it like a birth. That was not pleasant. The pain built again and I transcended again. It happened a couple more times before the final gong signified the end and I slowly fell over and eased my way out of position. Then, along with the others I walked out into the warm afternoon sun and all of us knew we'd changed.

So many retreats, so many hours of sitting, so alone, so lonely. It went on and on and I sunk deeper and deeper into the cave of my mind, the dark night of the soul. I stayed far away from women, was very definite about that. I didn't masturbate. There was no over-thinking it. I was as unwavering as I imagined the saints and sages of old had been in their own caves. I was as definite as I felt I needed to be, in search of answers to the great questions and personal power. I had no answers and I'm not sure I gained any personal power but it sure was getting interesting. What I did gain, however, from being so completely alone was a glimpse into the true nature of that aloneness and it fascinated me. Was I really alone? Was I even really lonely? What about that vision I had as a young unhappy kid, the one of the smiling bearded man? "Be patient," I'd heard him say, "and you will eventually find your real family."

Chapter 6

The Bullet I Dodged

During the first winter on Gabriola Island my only rent was to take care of my landlord's dog while they visited their families in Montreal. They were generously allowing me to stay in their lovely geodesic dome for the entire winter and all I needed was to do right by their dog. He was a skeletal white German Shepherd named, yes, Snowy. And Snowy needed a good meal. My landlords were strict vegetarians but I didn't think they should be taking it out on the mutt. He had a lean and hungry look that I found unsettling. So I immediately brought him a can of 'Kennel Rations' dog food which he inhaled in seconds. Next day I trotted off down to the island butcher shop because I decided to buy Snowy a juicy steak as a very special gift.

The dog ripped that slab of meat apart. He devoured it in a fashion that scared the bejeesus outta me. Later on, having developed a taste for blood, Snowy rather disingenuously decided to go after the neighbour's chickens. That was unfortunate. He was summarily shot and so within exactly two days of my occupying the house Snowy was gone. Ok he was dead. It was a peaceful winter. I saw no need to tell the people all the facts. Snowy was dead and wasn't coming back. All I said eventually was that he went missing and they concluded Snowy was crossing the country in search of them. Apparently the wife saw it in a dream and who was I to say otherwise?

There were a flurry of retreats, freelance articles and tree-planting contracts when I wasn't sitting alone somewhere on the island. After the dome I lived in a plastic lean-to, a tree-house, a couple of cabins, a camping trailer, even a chicken-coop. I did go to Hawaii one winter. I'd heard about a dormant volcano, called Haleakala, the quietest place on earth and according to my concept the perfect spot to meditate. Having landed in Honolulu I bedded down for the night in a park near the ocean, only to be awoken by a stringy guy leaning over me in the middle of the night. He was whispering something I could not decipher. Blurry-eyed I asked him to speak up but I still could not hear him. I asked him to speak up again but I still couldn't hear him. "Look man," I barked, "I can't hear you. Speak up." Then just barely loud enough I finally heard him say: "Do you want a blow-job?" And because I was so spiritual in those days I said: "Oh. No but thanks anyway."

By the next afternoon I was on the island of Maui where I eventually made my way to the volcano. It took me a few good hours to walk down to the bottom. A shack had been built there, perhaps as a trap for foolish aspirants like me who thought the perfect quietude was the key to gaining a lasting enlightenment. Certainly I could've heard a pin drop as I unrolled my mat. The cabin was a simple structure without glass or screens in the windows. I didn't take much notice of that fact until as I sat to meditate a couple of flies flew in and danced around like they were at the El Macombo on a hot Saturday night. In the stillness of that place they made a racket that was both incessant and maddening. I never knew flies could be so damn noisy. I tried to persevere but eventually I just left.

In a village not far from the volcano the very next day, I was sitting outside a store on a bench drinking some grape-juice when an earthquake struck. It was big. The whole board-walk started rippling. Trees began to sway dramatically. The bench seemed to rise off the ground. I was deeply involved in reading 'The Aquarian Gospel of Jesus the Christ' at the time. So perhaps since I'd never experienced an earthquake before or because I was ridiculously spiritual at the time, my first thought was that I was experiencing some sort of Kundalini opening. I closed my eyes. A few short moments later, noticing people running and screaming, I figured it out. Still I just waited, wondered how it would've been down at the bottom of Haleakala.

On the very last planting contract I went on that year, outside of Fort St. John, British Columbia, there was a lovely cook I dreamed about every night. Karen wore the loose-fitting cotton, flower-print dresses that west coast ladies liked so much in those days. Rather than hide her perfect figure it let me in, especially when the sun was behind her, and what I couldn't see I imagined. Karen was charming, fun, mischievous. In the truck she'd fiddle with the knob of the stick-shift and glance at me in the mirror. That was a tough one. I just wanted to finish that last contract and get the heck over to India while I could. I was on my way to meet S.N. Goenka, the world's main teacher of Vippassana meditation. But she was sooo lovely.

Back on Gabriola afterward as I packed for India, there was a knock on the door. Karen. It was Karen asking if I would teach her how to meditate. I'm sure many guys would've appreciated her interest in the ancient discipline of dhyaan yog meditation, but that evening I did not let her get even one toe inside the cabin. I didn't dare, told her I was too busy getting ready to leave and suggested she go see Param, a guy we had planted with who had only recently returned from India. His guru was Swami Shyam, in Kullu.

I knew several devotees of Swami Shyam on the islands. Two had come specifically to meet me for the first time earlier that very day. Gopal and his girlfriend Radha heard I was going to India and came to wish me well and to suggest I drop in to meet Swami Shyam up in the Himalayas. I wasn't listening. I was too busy checking out Radha. She was right up my alley, so to speak, around five-two, as cute as they come with beautiful, curly, blonde hair. She was playful, alluring. Hers was not just the beauty of youth. It was more of an ageless expression of her essence. I could hardly take my eyes off of her. All of a sudden I could hardly remember Karen as I looked at Radha. Luckily she was occupied, of course, I was strictly unoccupied and, really, I just had to get outta there. But Radha's smile would haunt me until we met again.

Once I made my way by plane to England I began a slow journey overland that lasted about two months and took me through many countries. I took a ferry down from Dover to Belgium, trains lurching through Europe, Greece, Italy, on and on. I spent a day, a week, or more in many places. There was a ride on the famous 'magic bus' through Turkey that was not magical at all. I hooked onto rickety local busses through Afghanistan where I shaved my head.

In Peshawar there were apparently no vacant rooms in any of the hotels available to non-Muslims and I was seriously knackered. Finally I was able to rent a horrible little rope cot on the over-crowded roof of an ancient hotel. With the cacophony of sounds, pungent odours and thick smoke of the market engulfing me, I sat to meditate out of need and habit without any confidence. That hellish place was the worst possible environment for meditation. It seemed futile and yet after an hour I realized that I felt entirely refreshed. As I walked around that roof-top actually appreciating the vibrant life all around, I remembered my ill-conceived trip to Haleakala in Hawaii and smiled to myself. One concept had just loosened its hold upon me.

When I arrived at the Khyber Pass I was told my medical papers were not in order. I waved my papers in front of the guard apoplectically to show that I had done all that was required but my protests fell on deaf ears. I had to return to Kabul where I received further inoculations with questionable syringes and made sure it was all noted on my papers before trying the border again. Once there I could not for the life of me understand why the same official was stubbornly saying the same things and refusing to let me through. That was, until I noticed how he kept staring at my relatively new shiny Nike high-top basketball shoes. As I pleaded with him I stepped out of my shoes and was then miraculously waved on. I walked shoeless through the border and onto a train to Amritsar.

As the rusty, crusty, dusty old train rumbled into the Amritsar station I noticed a Scottish guy slouched on a seat across the crowded isle slowly shaking his head. I had been watching him with interest for a while, exchanged hellos. He didn't look well at all and I perceived a growing anxiety in him the closer we came to the station. As we lurched to a final and abrupt stop he shot me a wry grin, screwed up his face and said he really couldn't 'fookin' believe he had to go back into 'fookin' India to renew his Afghani visa. Of course I was compelled to ask why he hated India so much, seeing as I had just spent months if not years looking forward to it. He said, "I loost me stoomik 'ere."

I had a fleeting and totally nonsensical mental image of him walking around all bent over searching for his stoomik but I would directly understand what he meant soon enough.

Meanwhile the moment I walked onto the platform and took my first steps on Indian soil I felt a sense of relaxation come over me. It was a visceral experience, palpable, undeniable and perhaps unexplainable. I've had the same feeling every time I've ever landed in India since. It certainly wasn't a logical reaction. I immediately started seeing red spittle all over the ground. I pondered the notion of India being a land of ulcers and tuberculosis. The red was beetle juice spat out as an integral part of the pervasive paan-eating ritual but I didn't know that then. I spent the first three nights sleeping in the famous, perhaps now infamous Sikh Golden Temple, in a plain cement room with a wide cross-section of humanity. In those days everyone was welcome.

On my third day in India I saw a man beating a water-buffalo mercilessly with a wooden cricket bat while a smaller man held it by its nose-ring and neck-rope. They were yelling while flogging the beast as it bellowed in pain. Nobody paid much attention until I grabbed the arm of the larger man and demanded that he stop. Then a crowd quickly formed around us and the two men screamed at me and at the crowd. There were a lot of histrionics I didn't understand until one willowy old man told me in English that the buffalo was very stubborn. I said that was no reason to beat it and then the two men did something I was not expecting. They handed me the rope and intimated that the buffalo was now mine. The two men stormed off, the crowd laughed, clapped and called out to each other while I stood frozen to the spot.

I was at a total loss, no idea what to do. Within three days of being in the country I found myself wandering through a market with a water-buffalo that, by the way, was indeed incredibly stubborn. It seemed singularly ungrateful to a guy who had just saved it from a heck of a thrashing. I hadn't gotten far when the willowy old man approached. Seeing me struggle he smilingly said, "You can do with that buffalo the same as so many problems in the life. Before you lose your good sense my son you can simply let it go." And that's exactly what I did.

Not long after arriving in India, in 1976, I decided to do a seven-day retreat at the Toshiba centre near McLeod Ganj above Dharmsala. Other than one aged monk, whose job it was to cook for me, I was totally alone. That was not the problem. The problem was that every time I opened my eyes I saw monkeys fornicating, everywhere, all over the damn place. Everywhere I looked there were monkeys doing it. I'm obviously no prude but that was ridiculous. So I left after only a couple of days, moved down to the 'Tibetan Library of Works and Archives'.

While at the library, taking in a few lectures by the Lamas was of course the thing to do. However, I refused to prostrate to them. That would be too much, I reasoned. So when the Lama would enter the hall and everyone else stood and then proceeded to prostrate flat out a few times each, I would pointedly, proudly remain seated. As a Vippassana bikku monk shunning all rites and rituals, prostrating seemed tremendously inappropriate.

I attended a lecture each morning and nobody cared that i refused to prostrate. After a few days, however, I at least began saluting the Lama with folded hands as if to say 'namaste.' Still there was no way I would actually prostrate. No way. But after another couple of days I stood, saluted and remained standing until the others finished their prostrations. That felt ok. I could do that. But then after about a week I decided there was no harm, and it'd be a more proper sign of respect to do a weee small half-prostration. Only, something happened during that weee half-prostration. Some rigid part of me let go, released, and i found myself flat out on the ground doing a full formal free frontal prostration along with everyone else, then another and another. I began to laugh in the middle of the routine. The Lama, watching me, began to laugh. Some of the others began to laugh. It was kinda wonderful. And as the days passed i realized that i looked forward to the prostrations more than the lectures.

By that time, while wandering around the village during those hot afternoons, watching the old Tibetans reciting mantra while fingering their mala beads, I wondered. I wondered about their trek across the mountains to save themselves and their kids, their beliefs, their way of life, to be free, to worship the way they knew. And once in a while I'd spin the prayer wheels in the temple at the top of the street.

Monkeys are a force to be reckoned with over there. The Toshiba retreat centre, for example, would regularly be taken over by monkeys whenever the place wasn't busy which, by the way, nobody bothered to tell me. As well, they do seem only concerned with feasting, fighting and fucking. And they're clever. One of the pack or herd stole my favourite western shirt off the railing over which I had draped it, wouldn't return the thing until I paid a handsome ransom in the form of fruit. Then, another stole a pair of my underwear. I told him to keep it but he threw it back anyway.

What bothered me and why i had left the retreat early was the overwhelming amount of sexual activity going on around me.

It was terrible, kind of disgusting. Obviously I just did not feel I should be meditating on monkeys rutting all around me, in the court-yard, on the walls, on my porch, even in the bathroom. They had no shame, no sense of decorum.

The last straw for me was when I found two doing it doggy-style on my bed. MY BED! I mean, why couldn't they get their own room? The place was empty. They could've had the friggin honeymoon suite. When I walked in and saw those monkeys on my bed I was so shocked I froze. The sight of their furry bodies slapping together rhythmically in a primal dance of life, well, I knew I had to go. Of course I waited for them to finish. While packing, however, I found myself wondering why that specific position was even named doggy-style. It might just as easily have been called the monkey-style. It's clearly their preferred style as well. Why do dogs get to be immortalized in that fashion when most animals and many humans like it best that way? Such were the quality of my thoughts as I threw the last of my things into the knapsack, a clear indication that my time there was done.

Satya Sai Baba once noted: "The mind is like a mad mischievous monkey flitting from branch to branch. We need to meditate and gain some control over that monkey."

Chapter 7

Kullu

After about a month in the area a German couple offered me a lift to Kullu and it occurred to me that that was where Swami Shyam lived. I recalled Gopal and Radha's visit the day before I left for India and thought I may as well go say hi to the swami, just as they had suggested. What the heck, right?

In those days the Kullu valley was pristine. There weren't many people around, almost no vehicles. The river was clean. It was a place where samadhi was dripping from the trees. The few houses seemed identical to one another and therefore as we approached the town a funky little pyramid made out of tin caught my eye. I knew that must be the place. So after I checked into 'The Fancy Guest House,' which wasn't, I wandered back up the road toward the ashram.

I felt an odd sense of excitement that was a little unsettling. After all, I had met many so-called masters, teachers and spiritual guides by then. It was not my first rodeo. As I started up the rough steps of the ashram I was met by a fellow who asked rather curtly what I wanted. His tone put me right off. I responded with a simple 'nothing,' turned on my heels and left. Later in the afternoon I was wandering in the bazaar, which was, when a western fellow strode right up, said I looked like a spiritual person and invited me to have a chai with him. It's not that he was tremendously perceptive. I was wearing saffron-colored kurta-pajama with mala beads around my neck, had a shaved head and I was walking with my hands behind my back. Anyway it turned out that Basant was from the ashram and, after I told him of the rather unwelcoming reception I received earlier, announced that he was going to set up a meeting with Shyam. Later that same evening, true to his word, Basant walked all the way back into town to inform me that Shyam would meet me at ten the next morning.

That next morning as I got ready to head off to the ashram I washed my face, then washed it again, washed it several more times in fact. At one point I looked at myself in the cracked, cloudy mirror and actually said, "What are you doing?" I was surprised and unsettled by the excitement, the sense of anticipation, even anxiety that rippled through me. Nevertheless I made my way over at the appointed hour and Basant was on the steps waiting. He led me up to where Shyam, which is also the name of the Supreme Being within the Hindu pantheon, was sitting in front of his little pyramid reading a book. As I was introduced he looked up over his glasses and said: "Oh what a clean, bright and shiny face you have." I was totally stunned, didn't know what to do. Then he locked me in his warm gaze and said: "Don't you remember me?" I was instantly transported back to when I was a sad, young child sitting alone in the garden. I remembered. I remembered how I had clearly seen in front of my eyes the disembodied face of a wise-looking, happy, bearded man. He had consoled me: "Don't worry. Be patient," he had said. "You will one day meet your true family."

I did remember but I didn't know or was not ready to accept who he was to me, this swami who wore eastern dhoti and western slippers. He ranted on about one all-permeating life, used words such as purity, freedom, eternity. He talked about how kids get screwed up by their elders, "...like young Nathan here just for example. Let's say he had a grade four teacher, old Mrs. Brown, who would smack him around when she'd catch him day-dreaming." The people sitting at the pyramid that day laughed out loud. I suppose it was funny. But it also happened to be true. "Stop your day-dreaming young man," old Mrs. Brown would holler between gritted teeth, eyes bulging, veins popping, barely under control, "unless you want to feel this stick again!" Shyam had succeeded in 'blowing my mind' completely and immediately.

As a Buddhist monk of course I was aware of the concept of 'no-self, shunya, void'. It had to be the same reality as the 'eternal, all-permeating self' that Shyam spoke of. Of course it had to be. Still I so preferred the very sound of 'eternal', so positive, so life-affirming. Swami Shyam's words washed over me like a flash flood wiping out whole unsuspecting Himalayan villages of my conceptual mind. How can we deny our very existence? Something cannot come out of nothingness. On the other hand I felt as though I was at the mad hatter's tea party. They were laughing way too hard, agreeing way too easily. And he wasn't talking. He was ranting.

A very short girl called Durga came along and immediately fell into a dead faint in front of Shyam. He dragged her onto his lap without stopping his discourse, pounded on her back to emphasize each point he made. Another girl, Madalsa, grinned at me like a Cheshire cat. Shyam knew what I was thinking, made that perfectly clear, left no doubt about it. Eventually he asked what my program was. I answered by saying that I just stopped in to say hello and meet him. He interrupted: "Many people come to meet Shyam but they don't ever get to know Shyam. If you want to actually know Shyam you have to stay for at least ten days and anyway you really need to rest."

I sort of ignored all that as I finished off by saying I was on my way to Bhod Gaya, the Maha Kumbh Mela and then the Vipassana centre in Igatpurri. He just shook his head, looked me straight in the eyes with an almost hurt expression and said: "Why are you doing all that when I'm right here?" Not bothering to wait for a response he asked how much I was paying at the 'Fancy Guest House', which wasn't. I told him I was paying seven rupees per night and he immediately said he would charge me six with meals. My thought at the time, believe it or not, was that it sounded like a fantastic deal. Shyam told a fellow called Bolay to show me to my room but as I walked away I heard him call after me: "Take it that if you do stay the whole ten days your life will change forever." I half-turned and muttered: "Whaaa?" but kept on walking.

Bolay showed me to a room in a place called Hill-House, which was in fact up the hill. Then he suggested we meditate for a while. That was fine only he sat rather close and facing me, which I found strange. Nevertheless we sat in silence for what felt like an awfully long time even for me. It was so long in fact that the room had become shrouded in darkness. I hadn't had any food or water all day. I really wasn't into sitting any longer but there was no way I was gonna let that guy out-sit me. I was a Vippassana Buddhist monk after all. I could sit in full-lotus posture for hours. So I continued to sit until eventually I heard Bolay say: "You are a bright star in the universe." Hard to know how to respond to that. If I recall correctly I simply said: "You too." Whatever the case may be, that was my first meeting with Shyam and my first day at the ashram.

Over the next ten days Shyam kind of wooed me. He romanced me without the sex. Men don't usually experience what I experienced during those days. It was magical, special, days I will never forget. The place was certainly unusual. That same small girl, Durga, would still fall in a dead faint every time she approached Shyam. Madalsa still smiled that inane, toothy smile. The laughter was still too loud. The women wore blue velvet gowns. The guys wore white kurta-pajama with mala beads. But there was clearly something remarkable happening there. And at the end of the ten days when Shyam asked me what my program was, I said I would just like to stay. He laughed and clapped his hands.

That's when everything began to unravel. Swami Shyam still loved me. He built me up but he also tore me down. He made fun of certain aspects of my personality, my concepts, my old patched-up running shoes, my Buddhism, even the way I meditated. We used to call it Shyam's crash course in enlightenment. Shyam seemed to take special delight in making fun of my shoes. It never occurred to me that I might explain how I lost my nice, new runners at the border or how I couldn't find any shoes in India near my size. He showed me a deep affection at times and would walk past as though I didn't exist at other times. I was finding the place to be a bit much, truth be told. Life at the ashram was beautiful. The days were filled with knowledge and magic. It was almost surreal. It was also constantly nerve-wracking, ego-challenging, confusing.

While sitting with Shyam at his pyramid one day in late December a letter arrived which he read with a sullen expression upon his face. When he finished, he flipped it onto my lap as though it was really meant for me. It was from Param. In the letter Param was informing Shyam that he'd made a girl, Karen, pregnant.

He was upset, didn't know what to do, felt as though his life was over. He said that all he really wanted was to return to India as a bramachari. He felt as though his hopes and dreams were shattered. I was totally shocked. I really was. It could've been me. It was supposed to have been me. I recalled the evening of Karen's visit, her flimsy flower-print dress, how she asked me to teach her meditation and how I suggested she go see Param. When I looked up from the letter Shyam was staring at me knowingly. He never said a thing about it but he knew.

After about two months I really had to leave. Life at the ashram was just too much for my nervous system. I was silently freaking out. I lied that I didn't want to leave but that I had committed to do a three-month silent Vippassana retreat. I could tell that Shyam knew the truth but he gracefully said that if it was hard to leave it'd be easy to come back. The day of my departure, just before going to catch the bus, I asked if he had any last-minute words of wisdom for me. He said yes, thought for a moment or two and then said something that has stayed with me ever since. "Don't be a Buddhist," he said, "be the Buddha." And with that advice ringing in my ears I slithered away.

Chapter 8

The Pathetic Little Thud

There were more than fifteen million people at the 1977 Maha Kumbha Mela. It was, according to the Guinness Book of World Records, the largest group in the world ever to assemble for a common purpose. It has been called the world's most massive act of faith. And in there somewhere among the Naga Babas, the mendicants, yogis and pilgrims, was I.

It had poured the night of my arrival, February 19, turning the whole of the mela on the banks of the Ganges at Ahallahabad into a giant mudslide. There was not a dry spot to lie down, no place to even sit. I walked with my bed-roll over my shoulders, for hours, just taking it all in. I saw a fellow who had been buried up to his neck for nine days. He spoke to me in English as I passed. I saw a baba that had held an arm straight up for years. It was stiff, withered. He wouldn't have been able to lower it if he tried. I wanted to shake his hand but… I walked and walked, watching the people, the animals, the life. A vibration of oneness was palpable. There was no meat, no drinking but plenty of smoking. It occurred to me that I would never see another spectacle to match the Maha Kumbha Mela ever again in this life.

Finally I really had to lie down. All that agitation and confusion I felt at the ashram in Kullu hadn't left my system. In fact I realized it was or had become something quite physical. I really didn't know what was happening to me. As I trudged along my mind and my tired, sick body seemed to finally give in. Worlds collided within me and I dropped down onto the muddy path. I actually felt a profound relief as I proceeded to leave the waking state and the walking state far behind. If I slept it was not a type of sleep I'd ever experienced before. I also had no memory of being carried. But when I regained consciousness I found myself among a group of yogis who were chanting, periodically ladling ghee onto a fire. It was surreal only I felt quite alright as I drifted off again. I thought of Shyam. I kind of missed him. I was aware of a real sense of freedom and personal power just from having known him.

The morning light brought me back. The mist created an otherworldly effect as I looked around and discovered that a bowl of yogurt and sweet jalabees had been placed beside me. I carefully tried a bit and the top of my head exploded with the wonder of it. I ate the whole bowl-full. It was amazing. I felt so much better. I jumped up, grabbed my dirt-encrusted blanket and with only a 'namaste' to the babas continued my wandering. As I walked through the crowds that morning with a renewed sense of well-being a young British couple came running up to me in a state of near-panic. They carried large packs, looked haggard and disoriented. The guy grabbed my arm and asked if I spoke English. When I said I did he quickly asked where the toilets were. I pointed to two parallel ropes that stretched for miles. "Anywhere between those ropes," was all I said. With a look of horror upon both their faces they faded back into the crowd.

There were processions in which groups would parade through the Mela. A guru would sit proudly atop a large elephant, disciples on smaller ones or running along beside. Some groups used carts. Some just walked. They also had varying degrees of pomp and circumstance. Those were the celebrations of India's long guru tradition and I rather enjoyed watching each, until one particularly lavish procession really caught my attention. It seemed too ostentatious, too grand. The guru sat high up on a mammoth pachyderm which was colorfully decorated with ornamental orange and red Rajasthani-style carpets, matching head-dress and bejeweled breast-plate. The man himself was quite large with a thick black beard, saffron robes and several rudraksh malas. Many smaller similarly decorated elephants followed behind carrying disciples while a throng of pilgrims flocked around that front elephant. They were trying to touch its tail, its feet, its trunk, with the belief that even one touch of the guru's own mount would wipe away all karmas.

The mahout was clearly frightened. The beast was side-stepping and twisting almost out of control. The great man however only laughed and wagged his finger down at the people, unconcerned, reveling in his glory. I couldn't help trotting along beside the massive skittish elephant. I knew people died regularly at the Kumbha Melas, trampled by a rush to bathe in the Ganges or, yes, under elephants' feet. I was caught up in the excitement of the moment not even knowing who the guru was. I only knew that I didn't like that he set himself so far up above everyone. Who did he think he was? He was clearly fearless but the whole scene seemed somehow wrong. What happened to oneness, one source, one all-permeating life force? Still I tried to keep pace with the frenzied crowd and the terror-stricken elephant when suddenly the great man turned right around in his howda, looked straight at me. I was frozen by the intensity of his gaze. 'Yes, you're right,' he said through his eyes, 'only don't tell me, tell them!' That was but a moment or two yet it stopped me in my tracks. He had spoken to me clearly. And as he rode off through the grounds he left me behind, amazed, dumbfounded.

That evening, I somehow found my way back to the camp I had been in the night before. It became my home base until I left the mela a few days later having made new friends, seen and experienced so much. It was a profound time along the path, without question, but was soon folded and put away into a corner of my mind once immersed again in meditation.

I sat for ten days with Joseph Goldstein and his Vippassana group under the famous Bodhi tree in Bodh Gaya, the very tree Gotam Buddha allegedly gained enlightenment while sitting under. I attended sessions with a Zen master there, Shabuyasung. We sat in an underground bunker-like room below his temple. I once asked if the void he talked about was akin to the sense of melancholy I often felt. Shabuyasung whacked me with his stick and told me to sit up straight. I listened to Thai monks and holy men and women of all sorts before heading south.

I waited in Gaya for a train during a hot-spell that was killing animals and people. The train was held up due to some sort of mechanical problem. Wandering around the market I was so hot my Kurta was drenched and sticking to my body. My head was swimming. I grabbed a Pepsi from a corner shop but of course it wasn't cold. Nevertheless I sat on a curb to drink it. The sun was beating down on me even though I was not sitting directly in sunlight. A bird fell from out of a tree and landed with a pathetic little thud right beside me. An old man, emaciated, dazed, wearing only a loincloth, stumbled around the corner and lay down in the street. He didn't fall. It was almost graceful. I don't know if he was dying. I just finished my Pepsi and got up. It was time for the train.

During the three-month Vippassana retreat in Igatpurri, I lived in a small mud and stone hut along with a small lethal scorpion. We co-existed without incident. My concept was that as long as I had only peace in my head and heart we would be fine. Luckily for me my bunkmate seemed to have the same concept. The days blended together in a silent march toward deeper and deeper levels of letting go.

I spoke with Goenka personally during that time when, in the middle of a moonlit night, he came to my hut to discuss tree-planting with me. He'd mistakenly assumed that because I had been a tree-planter by profession I actually knew how to plant trees. He wanted to place some in a specific place to block a view of funeral pyres down near the village of Igatpurri. It was great to finally get time with him but uncomfortable having to explain why being a tree-planter in Canada did not mean one would know anything about horticulture. "You see Goenkaji," I explained, "we were given bags stuffed full of saplings and paid according to how many we could shove in the ground during the day. We'd stick them in the earth as fast as possible every few feet with the hope that a decent percentage would somehow miraculously survive." Not surprisingly he found my description of the Canadian reforestation program pretty funny.

I spoke to him again during the last week. Our three-month retreat was as usual split into ten-day segments. Those of us who had been there the whole time sat closest to the front and to say we were deep in meditation by then would be an understatement. However, at the start of that final week Goenka beckoned me to sit directly in front of him. Once I sat down, hardly a foot away, he told me to close my eyes. Almost immediately I saw a brilliant sun shining within me and I felt a pulsating rapturous joy. It was not new to me but much deeper, brighter, stronger and more intoxicating than ever before. After about twenty minutes Goenka told me to open my eyes. When I did, all I saw was the same shimmering sun. His head had become the sun and shooting rays filled the room. "Do you see and feel the centre?" he asked. "YES!" I exclaimed. "From now on you will feel it. That will be your point of attention and you are an Arhart, stream-entry, no turning back." Then he simply told me to go back to my seat in the front row.

A couple of days later a tall, thin American guy, who had joined for that final ten-day session, flipped out. We were aware of him but paid little attention. I had seen it all before. He was quite sure Goenka was the devil and that we were all about to be served poison Kool-Aid and die. I have strong evidence now, all these years later, that suggests the sugar in the tea was rotting my teeth but otherwise it was pretty harmless. And if anyone had ever suggested leaving the sugar out I probably would've killed him or her myself. We're talking about serious sense-deprivation here don't forget.

The hapless fellow was so convinced that Goenka was the antichrist that he broke his vow of silence to try and save us. Of course it must've been disconcerting, even scary to plead with a bunch of silent slow-moving hulks that would not heed his warnings, pay attention or even acknowledge him. I was in the bathroom brushing my teeth that morning around 4:30 when he rushed in ranting about how Goenka had taken over our minds. The other people soon shuffled out but I continued to brush my teeth slowly, mindfully. I didn't see why I should cut it short. Brushing my teeth seemed like an orgy of sensual delight by then. I looked forward to it.

However, if it was unnerving to try pleading with a bunch of zombies who wouldn't look him in the eyes, it must've been downright freaky to try pleading with me. We looked at each other through the mirror while he ranted and I let gobs of toothpaste dribble down my chin. I grinned while nodding my head slowly up and down silently. He stopped, horrified. He looked at me with his mouth agape before turning 'round and running out into the darkness.

Soon after, we were all meditating in the hall, Goenka on his platform at the front. There was a silent ringing in the room, the sound of profound and utter stillness. Suddenly the American guy ran in yelling: "I have to save you! I have to save you!" It seemed to be happening somewhere far away or somewhere deep within my consciousness. I didn't even open my eyes until he was right in front of Goenka but by then it was too late. Goenka's eyes were still closed as the boy, yelling, raised a thick tree branch up high. However, just at that precise moment, as the club was about to plummet downward, Goenka looked up at him with a power that shot straight through as surely as if it had been a Taser. He stumbled backward, tripped on the step and fell in a heap sobbing, the club lying harmlessly beside him.

A couple of people ushered our would-be savior out and Goenka, in a loud booming voice commanded us to continue meditating. Everyone in the room had understandably been shaken. It was not peaceful. However, within a couple of minutes wave upon wave of 'shakti,' palpable deep profound peace, began to wash over us. It was dramatic. I felt as though I was being pushed backward by a warm, soothing, strong wind. It was unbelievable. Within another couple of minutes the space was back exactly where it had been before the interruption. When I recall that time and the look in Goenka's eyes I realize what that power was. It was love. I saw it clearly. I still see it clearly. It was love, compassion, and perhaps a tinge of concern. Mostly it was love.

Once the retreat ended and our vow of silence was lifted I was sitting on the door-step chatting with my neighbor when he spotted the scorpion. Fear shot through him and then for the very first time I saw my scorpion bunkmate become aggressive. It turned tail up and moved swiftly toward my neighbor who took off like a shot outta hell.

We were all leaving including Goenka but I wanted to say goodbye and thank him. After all, I knew that my time with him in Igatpurri would always remain a tremendous memory and a major milestone along my path. I waited outside his cabin for a long long time until he finally emerged. I quickly began: "Goenkaji I'm going back up to the mountains to be with Swami Shyam..." He interrupted me and positively barked: "I'm sure he's a very nice man BUT YOU CAN'T DO BOTH!" Then he straightened up, puffed out his chest and began to march to his car. I was stunned. I wanted to thank him. I wanted to say goodbye. I padded along, tried to keep pace, get another chance, but I smacked right into a tree and fell flat on my ass. Goenka did not even look back. He just got in his car, drove away and I never saw him again.

Chapter 9

She Left By The Back Door

There was never any question in my mind that I wanted to head back to Kullu at some point. Near the end of my time in Igatpurri, about eight months after I had slunk away from the ashram, I managed to send a letter asking Shyam's permission to return. I added a line that I later heard pleased him tremendously. I said that when I stepped off the bus it would be a disciple arriving. As it happened I very nearly fell off the bus.

In those days one had to ride twelve to fifteen hours in a rickety old bus, more if there were any mudslides, from Delhi to Kullu. By the time one reached the Pundho Pass in Himachal Pradesh, delirious, one's bobbing head would be systematically whacking the bar on the seat in front. The pervasive smell of onion garlic and body odor would make one swoon. Anyway, by the time I reached the valley again I was pretty well fried, nearly concussed, nauseous and nervous as if it were the first day at a new school.

Once the bus screeched to a stand-still I scampered up onto the roof to get my bag. My legs however had turned to rubber. My head was swimming. I was dizzy and unstable. So I grabbed for something, anything to hang onto. Clutching the arm of an old shepherd sitting up there I steadied myself while another guy actually held onto my ass-cheeks firmly. The bus driver honked, anxious to get moving on up the valley. I managed to find my satchel and threw it over the side; only my feet would not grip the ladder. I kept slipping. Precariously hanging from the top rung a third man reached down and held onto me while someone below guided me. Once I was on the ground the bus immediately rattled away. I collapsed onto my bag, my head in my hands, waiting.

I was in front of the local hotel, the only hotel near the ashram. It was a wooden ramshackle place in those days, owned by Pakistani Hindus who had settled there after Partition. One of the young sons came out and helped me. I got settled in a room, drank an incredible creation, from the mother of the family, made of hot milk with sugar, ginger and turmeric. I had a rest and then I felt like going to the ashram.

Shyam was lying down in his room playing a game of chess with a girl. I was amazed. That was Durga who used to faint every time she approached him. The room was lit by candles and the board was on Shyam's stomach. When he saw me Shyam immediately threw the board off, pieces flying everywhere, and shouted out my name. He pulled me down, placing my head in such a way that my ear was pressed to his chest. He began talking to the few people there about how he had always known that I would come back, about how I had undergone months more of tapasia, hardships, to purify my system and how I had been to the Kumbha Mela, Bhod Gaya, Igatpurri. At the same time, his heart seemed to be pounding right out of his chest. It was booming as though he was incredibly excited.

Eventually he pulled my head up, wiped my face lovingly with his hands. He said: "Be sure about your decision Mr.

Nathan. If you stay with me you will end up looking like me."
I responded by stating it would be an honor. Shyam laughed,
then simply told me to go meditate for a while in the hall and
as I left the room I saw him matter-of-factly begin another
game of chess with Durga.

I walked around as though in a dream for the next few days.
It felt so right to be back, at least for those next few days.
Then it all started over again. My nervous system began over-
loading. I recall sitting in a chair outside my room at Hill
House visibly shaking. On only about the third day back I was
already thinking I might have to leave. I wandered down to
the meditation hall and sat on a ledge overlooking the river.
A lady came out from Shyam's room and told me he wanted
me to go in. I really couldn't understand how he even knew I
was there but I walked to the hall, around to the other side and
knocked on Shyam's door.

In a loud voice Shyam called out, "Ouji ouji, Nathan, come in
come in." There were a few other people in the room and as
I sat down he resumed his discourse. He'd been talking about
complexes people carry with them like heavy bags through life,
only he began to use me as an example. I became consumed
by a pervasive paranoia, total insecurity. I wanted to run.
Interestingly, that was exactly what he was ranting on about, even
while the others laughed and shook their heads in agreement.
Bolay laughed so loudly at my discomfort that Shyam turned
to him. "Yeah, Bolay and I are together in this." Bolay stopped
laughing immediately and the color drained from his face.

Meanwhile I didn't think I could really take any more. I felt
as though I was closer to the cliff edge than when I had been
sitting outside on the ledge. Then Shyam went right up close

to my face with a few hand motions and well-chosen words that I don't even recall at all and he seemed to reach right into my head. It was as though he was turning the combination of a padlock. I actually felt a click, click, click in my head and then somehow I knew my life had changed, forever. Then he abruptly dismissed me. After meditating in the hall for a half hour I sat outside again, relieved, relaxed, content, happy. Shyam soon came prancing out with the others and made his way across the lawn. Seeing me he slowed long enough to ask how I was doing and I said I was fine. That was probably the most understated comment of my life.

By that time the number of people at the ashram had grown to about twenty-five. People kept coming and there were not really enough rooms. I stayed for approximately the next eight months, until the last of my money ran out. I needed to share my room with Gopal who had arrived, which drove me nuts. He was a good guy but always active, constantly chanting while fingering his mala beads or playing a chanting tape of Radha's over and over again. Her voice drove me nuts too but in quite a different way. I remembered her very well.

The days and nights blended together. In fact I often didn't know whether it was day or night, the time of day, even where I was. I was in another dimension. Only Gopal's relentless activity level kept me on the ground and I hung out more and more in the meditation hall. It was clear that I needed to talk to Shyam about my leaving. I had virtually no money, my shoes could not be patched in many more places, Gopal was driving me bonkers, Radha was chanting in my ears as though calling to me. It was time to go.

I tried to find the right moment to talk about it with Shyam. I was in the hall most of the time but it just never seemed right. He was busy supervising the renovations of the cow shed. Having had a big argument with his wife he had taken the cow, led her down right into his family's sitting room and began making the cow shed into his new home. There was a lot going on. I did not feel free to disturb him.

One day, sitting alone in the hall, looking at his door, I felt myself slip into a samadhi, a deep meditation. It seemed to descend upon me. I had to close my eyes. A thick column of intense bliss rose up through me to the top of my head while my conscious mind seemed to fade far into the background and dissolved altogether for some time. It was unexpected, incredible, profound, and lasted for about fifteen or twenty minutes. Immediately as the experience subsided Shyam's door shot open. He came bounding into the room, did a headstand right in front of me and then ran out onto the lawn and away.

Another day after sitting alone in the hall and again staring at Shyam's connecting door for a long time, I gave up and wandered outside. As I sat down on the ledge a lady called Pushpa came out of Shyam's back door, flushed, smiling beatifically. A minute later Shyam came striding out of his room by the front door. I didn't really think much of it. Of course the thought did occur to me that it looked like they had just had some sort of physical encounter. Pushpa just had 'that' look. Also, why would they come out of separate exits? Shyam surrounded himself with the ladies. That was a given, just as Krishna had played with the gopies. It was all good as far as we bramacharies were concerned. I'm quite sure I was one of the only guys to even entertain the possibility of Shyam having actual physical relations with one or more of them. But this was Swami Shyam, the one who could touch you on the forehead and put you in a state of consciousness no person would ever normally have. Needless to say I would inevitably revisit that issue later on.

In any event, I leapt up and asked if I could talk to him and after quickly explaining about sharing a room with Gopal and my lack of money, I said it just seemed that I'd meditate better back in Canada. He readily agreed, adding that I should go to the Shyam ashram house in Vancouver and get Bob to come to India. Having already been friends with Bob, lived with him on Gabriola Island, tree-planted beside him, I knew nobody could persuade the guy to do anything he didn't want to do. He was quite a head-strong kind of big, burly, beautiful red-headed guy who had already cancelled plans to travel to Kullu recently. When I mentioned all that to Shyam he pointed out that he'd take care of everything through me. I just had to go there. I really didn't understand it.

The day came for me to leave. There was a night-time satsang in the hall planned for until the bus was scheduled to pass by. Candles were lit, a tape recorder was placed in the midst of our circle and Shyam began to introduce all those present. I still did not have a Sanskrit spiritual name. I had waited and waited, not wanting to ask, and I was really scared he would once again just say my English name. He went around the room. I was the second-to-last person in the circle, the last being a lady who had only just arrived.

"This is Dayal," he began. "This is Meera. This is Praym. This is Malti. This is Durga. This is Bolay. This is Sukhdev. This is Gopal." As he turned to me Shyam announced, "and this is Hansraj." At the same time my kundalini shot straight up to the top of my head. My head actually hit the wall behind me. The rest of that evening became a blur. I don't recall the speeches or saying anything myself. I don't think I did say anything. I only remember repeating my new name inside my head over and over again like a mantra. I do remember hugging Shyam goodbye and then I walked up to the road, took my old patched-up running shoes off and left them on the doorstep of Shyam's new hut as a sign of my devotion and surrender. Then I jumped barefoot onto the waiting bus.

Chapter 10

Orgasms Are A Major Cause
of Babies

Kitsilano, Vancouver. The area was still funky. Banyan Books, the first exclusively spiritual New-Age bookstore in the country, was in an old clap-board house on Fourth Avenue. It had faded stained wing-back chairs, a meditation loft with threadbare carpets and mottled cushions. The Naam restaurant was equally funky, charming, THE place for vegetarians to eat in those days.

There was a weird, disparate, fun mix of folks living in the ashram house: Bob, Girdhar, Dev Kumar, Chandni, Lynn, Gagan, Allan and, yes, Radha, beautiful Radha. I was of course a little freaked out. Ok I was a lot freaked out. It felt as though she followed me from room to room. She probably didn't realize I was totally captivated by her long before ever landing there. When I first arrived all I could do was meditate. Sitting in the meditation room hour after hour, people would come and go but every time I opened my eyes there was Radha. In fact if she wasn't there it would feel as though something wasn't quite right.

After about a week Bob came in and proudly showed me the airline ticket he'd just bought. He was leaving immediately for

India, for Kullu, for Swami Shyam's ashram. Obviously I asked what made him change his mind. "Just watching you," he said. I didn't need him to elaborate. I was just amazed and bemused by the memory of Shyam's prophetic words: 'You don't have to do anything. I will do everything through you.'

Radha and I, along with one or two others, drove Bob to the airport a day later. Just before he went through the gate he asked if I had any message for Shyam. I looked at him, then down at Radha, curly blond hair, classic doe-like eyes, holding my arm, smiling up at me. "Yes," I said. "Please ask Shyam to help me, somehow, quickly." We all laughed but she and I crawled into bed together for the first time as soon as we got back to the house that evening, the first time I had sex in six years, the first time I ever really and truly made love in my life.

Radha was the love of my life. I knew that right away. Unfortunately I was not the love of her life. In retrospect I probably knew that right away too. I don't know what I was to her but it wasn't that. Those were some of the most wonderful and horrid moments I've ever known. I loved her deeply. Of course the truth unfolded over time. To be fair, Radha always insisted she didn't really want another relationship. She just wanted to go back to India. Her heart was in India. Now, of course, I understand how ridiculously impossible my situation really was. At the time, well, we did end up living together for the next many months. I thought I at least had a chance.

We rented a charming flat in an old carriage-house that overlooked Kitsilano Bay. We watched the tall ships float in and out of the harbor. I waited for her after work. We slept together every night. In fact I couldn't imagine sleeping without her. When she asked if I minded losing my ojas I'd say I wasn't losing it if I was giving it to her. That's the way I honestly felt. We never talked about Gopal. His name was never mentioned. However she did mutter 'Shyam' once at a climactic moment during sex. That was mildly unsettling at the time and makes much more sense to me now.

About two months of my being back in Canada someone returned from Kullu with a bunch of photos. In the pile were a series showing Shyam doing 'pooja', (a ceremony of honour,) over my old patched-up running shoes, the ones he used to make fun of, the ones I secretly placed on his doorstep the night I left. He had placed them on a fancy silver thali tray. His hands were folded as a form of respect. Seeing those pictures touched me, reached right in to my heart and transported me back to India, Kullu, to him.

Sometimes being in Vancouver, working as a house-painter, living with Radha, I marvelled at what a turn my life had taken. I would flash back to the falcons on the Mexican cliffs, the Jesuit minister in that Sierra Nevada mountain retreat, that last migraine with Ruth Dennison in Oregon, the Maha Kumbha Mela, Goenka, Shyam, the rishis I had met along the way. It was such a totally different reality. My whole world had somehow shrunk as I became more and more wrapped up with one girl, who clearly wasn't even sure she wanted to be wrapped up with me.

As the months passed I felt as though I was living with two people. Radha could be fun, loving and considerate one minute, then serious, cold and uncaring the next. One night as we were in the throes of passion Radha began to shake. She began to rattle and roll. I wasn't doing anything particularly new or different but her mouth fell open, eyes rolled in her head, back arched. I knew the signs. Her stomach began to contract. Her breath became more guttural. It was happening, finally. But then she stopped herself. She just stopped, flat out refused to let herself have an orgasm. Back then, well, I was still a young idiot, didn't really know what I was doing, could've made it happen I suppose. But I just felt she simply didn't want to surrender to me, to us. And that may well have been true. It was true. Only that wasn't her story. Radha insisted she got scared, thought she'd been about to conceive.

Our relationship changed after that or I changed. Since she had held her leaving for India over my head for nine months I gave her the last of the money she needed. I had next to no money but I simply had to force a decision. Maybe that was stupid of me, and those last weeks together were pretty rough on both of us. I totally didn't want her to go and she was as always of two minds. She held tightly to her decision and yet, the very day before her flight, she called from downtown to say she'd found a perfect carpet for the living room. When I reminded her of her imminent departure she cried. She cried a lot but she did leave.

I told Radha often that I loved her. She would never say it to me of course. She would never have been able to even consider leaving had she allowed herself to feel remotely the same. I predicted that if she stayed a year in Kullu I would be arriving there just as she was leaving. There didn't seem anything I could do. She had begun her journey to the land beyond men, or at least beyond me. In the end, as Radha walked along the glassed-in corridor to her waiting plane, red- eyed, not wanting to look at me, I strode along until she went through the gate. Then I sat down on a bench and, for the only time in my adult life, maybe in my whole life, I wept uncontrollably, like a baby.

Radha spent the next few days in Montreal with her family and we talked every day. By and large those conversations were continuations of the same prolonged argument we'd been having for weeks, months. My very last words before her flight to India were: "If you stay only four months or less I'll marry you when you get back." And her very last words to me were: "That's what I'm thinking." Somehow however I knew I'd lost her. Up until the moment Radha boarded that India-bound plane all the buckets of semen I had poured into her felt like deposits in a joint bank account. As soon as that plane took off I felt as though the manager had just run off with the money. The doors closed. I was penniless, out in the street. I couldn't sleep. I walked and walked. I could hardly eat, rolled my head around on tree-trunks, cried. I was inconsolable.

It was actually kind of interesting, in a tragic sort of way. As long as we were in love, as long as oneness was being served, as long as there was even a hope of unity, it was all good. But once Radha made her choice and left, once we split up, the reality was horrible. My well-being had become, in effect, dependent upon someone else. Such is the very nature of attachment.

I walked alone. I waited for word from her, of her. Weeks passed and all I heard was that Radha had made light of the situation to Shyam when she first arrived. Finally I received two letters, though neither was from her. They were from Shyam. One was an aerogramme written in his own hand-writing. The other was one he had dictated to Radha to send to me. In the aerogramme, written on 14/2/1977, he wrote: "Dearest Hansraj: Whenever I remember you, I am connected with my own consciousness. You are so brilliant that you always attract me. But you are so dumb to have loved a woman who never responds to you very kindly..." He mentioned two telegrams I had sent and how people talked about the whole affair in a very 'disarming' way, how lucky I was to remain free of wife and children.

The letter he dictated to Radha the next day was quite different: "Dearest Hansraj: Radha is here now, very safe, sound and glowing with the radiance of the absolute knowledge. Boy, you can never reach her. It must be very frustrating. She is much grounded and always remembers the whole that encompasses every being. So you are always there as I am always there with you. She got two telegrams but she did not stir a bit. I said, 'What for the telegrams are?' She said, 'Telegrams are just for telegrams' sake'..." The rest was just about how he loved me and so forth.

That was pretty much it for me. I did end up arriving back at the ashram just as Radha was leaving but she returned within another year, forever. I was there for much of the time, twenty-five years. We kept a respectful distance, never really talked, never really connected. We've always in fact remained uncomfortable in each other's company. She has been with the same guy now for many years, Shyam's right-hand-sort-of guy. I've been married and divorced. I now live in Canada but she still sneaks into my thoughts and dreams now and then.

Chapter 11

Zombies Are Only Human

After Radha left it was a slow climb back up. My spirits hovered around my ankles for a heck of a long time. Luckily I was always able to rely upon my loving family for understanding and support. Er, well, at least I had a few good friends around. Er, well, at least one friend was so kind as to come over, take her clothes off and jump into bed with me. Lynn was a sexy exotic dancer who had only recently been introduced to meditation by Dev Kumar, who was willing, even eager, to teach her all about oneness. Since Dev eventually left for India around the same time as Radha it seemed only natural to Lynn that we console each other. She had a body that could console just about any guy, except me. I could not even think of it. I told her I just wasn't into 'it', gave her a hug and was left to continue picking up the pieces.

There was a flyer tacked up in 'Banyan Books' advertising a three-day Vippassana retreat on Vancouver Island with Ruth Dennison. I heard that Goenka excommunicated her from the U Ba Kin lineage due to some unorthodox teaching methods she had begun using in her retreats. Robert Hover had also been excommunicated, for getting it on with one or two of his students. The timing could not have been better for me to take a 'time-out'. As well, I hadn't seen the old girl in years. It was somewhat deflating therefore when Madam Dennison showed no signs of remembering me at all.

Nevertheless the retreat began as they all did: in silence, endless hours of meditation with only 'sati pitana,' mindful walking meditation to break the monotony, although that was in itself monotonous. In fact, except for the unusual brevity of the retreat, I really couldn't understand what was so different from the norm. That changed when we were instructed to pair off for a short mutual massage session in the early afternoon of the second day. That was weird enough but what came soon after that blew my mind. Ms. Dennison told us to go out onto the front lawn of the place.

Once outside she told us to fly around as though we were butterflies. I really couldn't believe it. That was so not like any Vippassana retreat I had ever been to. I was consumed by a mixture of surprise, indignation and terror. I thought: 'I am a long-time Vippassana meditator. I've sat with Goenka for months on end. This is totally undignified and I will have to refuse.' At the same time everyone else began to circle the yard. So I felt I had no choice. I really had no choice. I let go, joined in, slowly at first. But as soon as I started flapping my arms like a butterfly I began to laugh. I laughed harder than I had in many months. I glided around the yard flapping, laughing and feeling the soft moist grass under my feet and the warm afternoon air on my face. That was truly an amazing few minutes during what turned out to be an amazing meditation retreat. Ruth Dennison may have been thrown out of that lineage of Vippassana masters but she certainly managed to teach at least one very serious meditator how to fly.

I felt much better after that time with Madam Dennison. Right afterward I met a funny fellow in a coffee shop back in Vancouver. Ray said we had gone to summer camp together years earlier in northern Ontario. I didn't really recall but I remembered his older brother. As well, he told me Angie, the first girl I ever saw naked, had died. Tragically, almost ironically, she died of breast cancer. So, yeah, Ray had obviously been there. He had also recently broken up with his girlfriend, was in a profession he hated and frankly he didn't seem very healthy. But he was terribly entertaining and we started hanging out. I taught him to meditate and he kept me laughing. His dream was to be a stand-up comic and he was darn good. Eventually, actually against my advice, Ray decided he just had to go to India, to meditate with Swami Shyam. And not long after he left I received this memorable letter from my mom:

Nathan; I had a telephone call today that upset me very much from a Mrs. Firestone. She was crying on the telephone because of what is happening to her son. What makes you think that you have the right to convert a good boy into a zombie, and then send him to India to become a convert to your way of life?! When are you going to wake up to realize that you are brainwashed into a totally unrealistic world? You are, if nothing else, starving yourself and you are going to kill yourself from malnutrition. No one can exist without food, not even you, because no matter how your mind tells you otherwise, your body is a machine that needs certain things like food at several intervals a day. Why can't you shake yourself out of the lethargy you have enveloped yourself into and come alive to know what you are doing to yourself? The dictionary gives this meaning to the word zombie: 'someone little smarter or livelier than a corpse,' or 'the body of a dead person given the semblance of life by a supernatural source.' If that is what you want for yourself, okay, but for all that is good in this life and for the sake of a family, keep your influence off another human being! I don't know who was responsible for you becoming what you are, but I don't want you being responsible for doing it to another human being. I am no longer going to accept or condone something that is reprehensible to me and from now on I am going to tell you exactly how I feel and in this way I hope to be able to snap you out of the horrible wasted life you are leading. Wake up before it is too late and you are so wasted away that you will be unable to regain health and vitality. Don't waste what had all the earmarks of a good and useful life. Come home and let us help you regain what you have lost!

Mother

I could always count on dear old mom for that kind of understanding and support. The simple truth is I hadn't seen or spoken to her in years so she really didn't know much about what I was doing. Ray loved India, Shyam and being at the ashram. He stayed for about four months. However he was diagnosed with testicular cancer not long after his return to Canada. I was in India again by then.

Ray had the operation, the chemo; he went through the whole procedure and seemed to progress well. Once he was better his parents urged him to get back to work. He did but the cancer soon returned. He likes to call that period his last ball. The doctors were not optimistic. He wrote to ask Shyam if he could go back to India, to the ashram, to die there. Shyam said no, that he could only come if he intended to live. So of course he left for

India almost immediately. Then almost immediately Shyam sent Ray and I to an Aryuvedic hospital in Denanagar, near Amritsar in the Punjab. Run by a very aged Swami, Swami Sarvanand, the place was famous for its non-invasive successes with cancer patients. The Swami was said to have miraculous healing powers.

That was at a time when there was tremendous unrest in the Punjab. Kalastani Sikh separatists were causing a lot of trouble, travelling through the district was dangerous but we had no problem along the way. Swami Sarvanand greeted us but he would not look at Ray, not even a glance. He talked to us with the help of an interpreter; he ate lunch with us, prescribed herbs and made a follow-up appointment, all without ever once looking directly at Ray. We were there several hours and just before we left Ray asked the Swami if he had any last words of advice. Swami Sarvanand then looked directly at Ray for the first and only time and in pretty good English he said: "Give up this hope you have of dying. You are not going to die." Ray was visibly shaken. I pushed him into our taxi and we headed back to Kullu. You might say we had a Ray of hope.

Over the next couple months Ray seemed to be fine. He took his herbs religiously, even drank the cow urine daily which Swami Sarvanand had insisted upon. He returned to Denanagar a couple more times and the world was as it should've been, for a while. When Ray's health began to deteriorate almost overnight a couple of allopathic doctors and one homeopathic doctor were brought in and the whole community was buzzing with concern. Nobody had ever died at the ashram. Nobody could imagine such a thing, although all three doctors agreed Ray was on his way out, so to speak. That being the case Ray just wanted to take morphine, watch videos and eat chocolate. The folks around him insisted he read scriptures, meditate and only watch videos of Shyam's discourses.

Eventually someone brought the issue up to Shyam and he said Ray should be free to do whatever he wanted and that he wasn't going to die. Ray sent a note asking for clarification: "Do you mean that philosophically, eg: the Self is eternal, or that my body will be carrying on?" Since I was the one delivering the note I witnessed Shyam's sheer delight at reading the note but he didn't respond. Some people, including all three doctors, were of the opinion that Ray should just give up, keep taking morphine and accept that he had reached the end. I was of the opinion that Shyam would not appreciate him merely giving up, that he had come to the ashram to fight for the life. Meanwhile, while that discussion was raging around him, Ray's parents had been calling again and again which was not easy in those days. There was only one phone in the whole ashram area and long-distance calls were most often unsuccessful. They were understandably upset, begging him to go home. Shyam soon suggested he listen to his family.

As soon as Ray landed in Canada he was whisked off to the hospital. However not one sign of the cancer could be found in his body. That news took everyone back at the ashram by complete surprise. The doctors were shocked, embarrassed. One of them exclaimed to me: "But he had all the signs!" To which I responded somewhat patronizingly: "I guess you should always hold out for the possibility of a miracle." Many people credited Swami Shyam. Many people credited Swami Sarvanand. All I know is I've never been able to think of cow urine in quite the same way. Ray has been alive and doing well ever since. He became a relatively famous stand-up comic, was a regular on late-night talk shows for some years, a writer of sitcoms. And he's been to the ashram several times since.

Chapter 12

That's a Muscle Too

When I was living on that beach in Mexico so many years before, when I would body-surf, when the force of a wave would throw me under and whip me around, I had a system. I would find a little room at the bottom of the ocean. I wouldn't struggle. I'd wait for the big bad wave to pass over and once it seemed like the coast was clear I'd resurface, ready for the next. While I was in that little room I'd just be with me. In fact I would just be. And sometimes there was no 'would just be.' There was simply 'I' alone. Words cannot go there, in that little room. I can't say where the waves come from or where they go. I can't say where the thoughts come from or where they go, where I come from before the body and where I'll go after. What I know is that there is a room at the bottom of the ocean of life which is pure and free.

Eckhart Tolle wrote in 'Eckhart Tolle and Egoless Sex': "When you are no longer totally identified with forms, consciousness, who you are becomes freed from its imprisonment in form. This freedom comes as stillness, a subtle peace deep within you, even in the face of something seemingly bad. This, too, will pass. Suddenly, there is space around the event. There is also space around the emotional highs and lows, even around pain. And above all, there is space between your thoughts. And from that space emanates a peace that is not 'of this world,' because this world is form, and the peace is space. This is the peace of God.

"Now you can enjoy and honor the things of this world without giving them an importance and significance they don't have. You can participate in the dance of creation and be active without attachment to outcome and without placing unreasonable demands upon the world: fulfill me, make me happy, make me feel safe, tell me who I am. The world cannot give you those things, and when you no longer have such expectations, all self-created suffering comes to an end. All such suffering is due to an overvaluation of form and an unawareness of the dimension of inner space. When that dimension is present in your life, you can enjoy things, experiences, and the pleasures of the senses without losing yourself in them, without inner attachment to them, that is to say, without becoming addicted to the world."

I'm not comfortable with the word 'God' but I do love that quote by Tolle. Be that as it may, it's impossible to always stay so free. It's also impossible, at least for me, to stay outta trouble a hundred percent of the time. I say wrong things sometimes, write wrong things sometimes. Sure I do. I swallow my foot, so to speak. More than sixty-five years in this body, approximately forty-five years meditating and I still get into trouble. All that to say I once got into trouble by saying I knew Shyam had sexual relations with the ladies. Oops.

In retrospect I understand that was a wee bit of a politically incorrect and unfortunate choice of things to blurt out. It was in the course of an innocent private conversation with two buddies as we walked along the road. I didn't think anything of it until I was summoned to a meeting with Shyam the next day, and even then. I had no idea my comment had been a revelation to one of those guys or that it hit him hard. He complained to his girlfriend who in turn ran to Shyam. I was quite happy to have been invited to a tea party with Shyam. I got all nicely suited and booted and rushed down to the ashram, oblivious of what was waiting for me.

There were about five of us invited or summoned to the meeting but I was the first to arrive, eager as I was. Shyam started haranguing me immediately. Of course then I realized it was not a friendly get-together. It was not friendly at all. He was clearly upset, practically yelling. At one point before the others arrived he barked: "If it's just a rumor, as you've said, why you accepted it as true?!" "Well," I stammered, "I accepted it as true and then checked myself to see how I felt about it, about you, and I felt fine. I thought it was better than putting my head in the sand." He seemed to like that answer. He even smiled for a moment.

Of course, I didn't feel so totally fine about it but I was in self-preservation mode in that moment. Of course I didn't actually know directly anything. Still, in truth that issue was confusing complicated, not simple, not then, not now.

Be that as it may, as soon as the others filed in the atmosphere became really quite dark. Shyam was on fire. We were all shaking in our boots, or sandals as it were. I was of course the central figure in the drama but nobody escaped his wrath. Devi, my best friend in those days and even all these years later, albeit before reading this book, was labeled as the rumor-monger, a probable source since she had been very close to Shyam for years. I defended her, insisted that she had nothing whatsoever to do with the whole sordid affair, excuse the expression. As a former journalist I had a vague understanding that one never discloses ones sources. My source did add, however, the curious statement: "I don't know what it was, but it wasn't exactly sex."

In my own feeble defense I insisted that my remarks had been misconstrued, misunderstood and taken out of context. The fellow who had gotten his knickers all in a twist by my remarks interjected at that point: "I don't wanna call Hansraj a liar," he so generously offered, "but he did say it exactly that way." This of course meant that he was in fact calling me a liar. Fair enough I suppose, but we haven't remained bosom buddies. Also, even during the proceedings I kept thinking that I pretty much knew the rumors were true and that the whole situation was bullshit. At the same time I did not believe for a moment that Shyam was now going to hate me, although it sure seemed like it.

In the end he announced: "OK, we know who the culprit is here and who spreads bad stories." Everyone looked at me with beady, accusatory, hate-filled eyes. "I don't ever want to hear another word about it!" And with that we were dismissed.

Everyone beetled out as quickly as possible. Since I was the first to enter I was the last to leave. Shyam, walking behind me, was still ranting. He was hollering. "I work damn hard! I don't deserve this! I don't need this sort of trouble! I work day and night and what I need is my muscles massaged at the end of a long day!" Then as he turned to go into his room he added just loud enough for only me to hear: "And that's a muscle too." I stopped, looked around. He was laughing as the door closed behind him.

Later that same night I decided to go down to the ashram. The hall was pretty full and I nestled in near the middle, comfortably lost in the crowd. Shyam entered eventually and sat on his platform at the front. However, as he occasionally did at night, he got off his seat and had cushions put down on the ground for him like the rest of us, against the wall, in the middle. So suddenly I found myself in the very front row hardly two feet from him. That was weird considering what had transpired earlier. I squirmed. Then I simply decided I'd get up and leave if the situation became too awkward. It's a big world out there, I kept thinking.

At first it certainly seemed as though I should leave. It actually seemed as though I should check the bus schedule. He was in a joking mood but he wouldn't look at me. He'd look at everyone around me but not me. I was definitely weighing my options. However, before I made a move to get up he said something that struck me as especially funny and I laughed. I don't recall what it was but I laughed and everything changed then. He looked right at me and laughed too. Then it seemed as though we were alone in the hall for the rest of the evening. He seemed to be in a really good mood. I asked questions. We laughed. Although I don't recall anything specific that we discussed during that satsang, in my memory it remains one of my favourite, most enjoyable ones of all time. Interestingly, the friend who had ratted on me didn't come out of his hole for several days.

For a short while around that time, Shyam made a rule that all ladies who wanted to go to his chalet in the evening had to pay. They'd hand over their fifteen rupees at Maya's cottage, receive a ticket, and then parade all together up the steps to the chalet. One night I was playing chess with my friend Dayal in his cottage, which was next to Maya's, when the ladies began their march up the steps. So I called out: "It's only ten rupees in here!", which I thought was spectacularly funny. Nobody else, however, seemed to find it the least bit funny and Dayal uttered something about me perhaps learning to keep my big mouth shut.

On one of those other-worldly Himalayan mornings the rains subsided leaving only a haze drifting across the mountains, along the slopes, in the gullies. The grass seemed greener, the air perhaps more fresh. It was a crisp New Year's Day and we were all invited on a trip with Shyam.

We drove in a convoy up the valley, many Hindustani Motors Ambassador cars snaking their way through villages and towns to the fancy new 'Span Resort Hotel'. The villagers and townspeople were out after the intense monsoon deluge watching us with interest all along the way until we disappeared through the large, freshly painted, green hotel gates. Owned by one of the most prominent members of the national assembly at the time, the erstwhile Mr. Kamul Nath, the valley had never known any place quite like it. A lavish stage had been prepared in the luxurious dining-hall in front of the picture windows that looked out over the fast-flowing Beas River. There was a high padded seat for Shyam covered in brocade cloth. A video camera was set up, a speaker's chair placed to one side and plenty of flowers. Politicians were there, the king of Kullu, Kamul Nath's family, some wealthy hotel guests and of course all of us.

Speaking into a video camera was new to Shyam but he took to it naturally. He loved it, was having almost every occasion recorded wherever he went. Once the session began Shyam talked for a while, praising the new hotel and its creator, then called others to speak, giving each person a glowing introduction. Meanwhile coffee, tea and pakoras were handed out by servers in crisp red uniforms. But it was not my cup of tea. I decided the room was too full of stuffed-shirts. It was too formal, too predictable. I actually became more and more irritated. Honestly I was really getting upset that my name was not called.

Finally I'd had enough. I wandered out of the hall then up the winding stairs to the lavatory. I stood at a sparkling white marble urinal and began to piss. All of a sudden Shyam flung the door open, rushed in, went to the urinal beside me. It shocked the heck outta me. I had been entertaining some pretty nasty thoughts and his sudden presence threw me for a loop. Also, although he could've used the urinal further away, which any normal guy woulda done, he chose the one right smack dab beside me.

Neither of us spoke for a moment or two. "Swamiji," I finally said, "since you came in my pee has stopped." He chuckled and said, "Never mind, gimme a kiss." I'm afraid however that the thought of leaning over and kissing my guru while both of us were holding our dicks was a little too much for me. It was just too friggin weird. I did lean over toward him. He was clearly ready and waiting to plant a big one right on my lips. But at the last second I turned away and Shyam kissed my cheek. Then he grabbed my head and stuck his tongue deep into my ear. He laughed uproariously as he shook the last drops from his penis, pranced out of the bathroom still laughing and I had to sit down on a toilet for a while.

At the conclusion of the hotel visit we thought that was that but it wasn't that. It wasn't that at all. Shyam's car turned north and so our car turned north, heading further up the valley to the snow. Twenty minutes later we walked through a forest and of course a video was made of Shyam discoursing while standing in the snow without a shirt. Then we walked on until we found a green spot where another video was made while Shyam leaned against a tree, again without his shirt. He asked me to take his boots off and put his shoes on, which I attempted to do as he continued to talk.

Taking his boots off did not present a problem. They were pretty loose. I knelt on the ground out of view of the camera, slipped one boot off but it was difficult to get the shoe on. Without stopping his speech Shyam pushed and pushed and I pushed and pushed, eventually getting the damn thing on. It was not easy. I slipped the other boot off but the other shoe was even harder to get on. He pushed and I pushed. I pushed and he pushed. It was not going on. Then he pushed so hard that he forced my hand to the ground and, as luck would have it, right into a heaping pile of cow shit. He kept pushing my hand into the shit while saying, "This is going to be Hansraj's special year." This would've normally really warmed my heart, if he hadn't been mashing my hand deeply into cow shit at the same time. The camera panned down to get a shot of me smiling adoringly up at him even while my hand was buried in crap out of the camera's view. Afterward people congratulated me on having been so blessed by Shyam as I kept that hand behind my back waiting for an opportunity to wash it in the snow.

Shyam had fallen in love with the video camera. It was entirely consensual. The camera loved him back. He had videos made of every occasion. For example, at that same time the Health Minister for the province of Himachal Pradesh visited the ashram and Shyam insisted the satsang be videoed. I was sitting in the front row and could clearly see the ashram dog Tipoo sleeping under Shyam's platform, as she often did. It would look bad if the minister saw that. A dog allowed in a house or a common room was considered really quite unhygienic which, if you think about it, it is. The lady beside me kept whispering that I should go up and grab her. Of course then the minister would've certainly seen that we basically lived with a dog. People around us were murmuring, twittering, beginning to chuckle. Wonderful speeches were going on even while many of us were having trouble keeping a straight face. Then it happened. Tipoo wandered out from under Shyam's platform, stretched lazily and dragged her ass across the carpet before stopping to lick her genital area right in front of the Minister of Health. That was terrible, terrible, and I loved it.

One of the first things Shyam ever said to me was that I should not smoke dope or take any drugs. He said I needed to repair my nervous system and he made me promise to stay 'clean' for seven years. That was an easy promise since I actually had already stopped, everything, when I had become a monk in California.

Years later Rutna, a retired school master who used to attend satsang daily, had a heart-attack or a stroke or something right at the ashram. He left the hall, stumbled into an adjoining room and Shyam instructed Hanuman and I to go see what was happening. Soon, with Hanuman and I beside him, Rutna was breathing hard and Shyam came in. He stood over Rutna, nonchalantly straightening his shawls. Rutna was trying to talk but Shyam kept repeating: "Don't worry, just let go. Don't worry, you've done absolutely everything. Just go, be free."

Divesh, Hanuman and I took the old guy to the hospital. But they left me sitting there while they supposedly went off to inform the family. Nobody came for a couple of hours as Rutna breathed his last. Finally, although I was pretty pissed off for having been abandoned, the three of us went together to report to Shyam who we found on the ashram steps. After informing him of Rutna's death, to my utter amazement he said: "Let's go to my room and smoke a joint." That's also when it dawned on me that it had been seven years exactly, to the day, since Shyam made me promise not to do any drugs.

Once we were sitting in Shyam's room with a couple of ladies joining as well, Divesh produced a small thin joint, lit it, and passed it around. I was last before Shyam to get the reefer and I guess I figured that, if I'm gonna take one toke after about nine years, it's gotta be a good one. It sure wasn't going around twice. So I sucked on that thing probably longer than 'normal' until I heard Shyam say: "You're bogarting." Everyone laughed at that while I thought: 'Bogarting? How do you even know that word?' Passing it over, Shyam took the tiniest fastest toke I'd ever seen before throwing it into his cup of tea.

Although I couldn't imagine anyone getting stoned off the size toke Shyam took he sure acted like he was: crazier, madder than like ever, which is saying a lot. He had everyone howling from his antics: throwing water from his pitcher onto peoples' heads, flinging pieces of oranges around the room, and so on. Meanwhile in sharp contrast to all that, I had slipped into a weird all-consuming mixture of paranoia and catatonia. While everyone was hooting and howling I sat rigid, stone-faced and deep within my own thoughts. At one point Shyam turned to me and asked: "What the heck's wrong with you?" To which I replied... nothing. I said absolutely nothing at all. I just sat there rigid, stone-faced, deep within my own thoughts.

The whole ashram was waiting in the hall for the evening satsang so Shyam took that moment to go and I was left sitting alone. I could hear what was happening: basically a continuation of what had been going on in his room, on a grander scale. It was raucous, wild and insane. I really didn't wanna go but I didn't really wanna stay either. So eventually I positively snuck or slithered into the very back of the hall. I hid behind everyone in the corner while Shyam continued to joke, throw things and act like the madman he was. Until at one point he stopped and announced in a big booming voice: "OH LOOK HOW BLESSED HANSRAJ IS TODAY." And approximately seventy-five people turned around to look at me.

I guess it was around that time I got scooped up by Shyam one early morning for a drive up to the high Himalayan village of Kothi. There was only Divesh, who used to drive Shyam, and myself. What was supposed to be a nice day trip, however, turned into a three-day retreat because of an unexpected snow-storm. We were totally stranded at the little guest-house, and it was amazing.

For three days we chatted, meditated, drank chai, ate dhal with rice, chatted and meditated with guru. Days and nights blended together as one transcendent experience, beyond anything that could be considered normal. I really felt fortunate to have that time with Shyam, and upon our return of course people wanted to hear about it. Almost immediately I found myself at a tea-stall with a bunch of friends proudly describing the beauty and majesty of the previous three days.

At the same time as my telling everyone about the bliss of the meditations and the richness of our satsangs, a guy nearby on a motorcycle was revving his engine. I called over to ask him to cut it out but he didn't. I was in the midst of talking about one meditation with Shyam specifically that took us to a depth of samadhi that could only be described as remarkable but that guy kept revving his engine.

Eventually I got up, went over and told him to either cut his engine or leave. He looked me straight in the eyes and revved his engine longer and louder than ever. I went berserk. I grabbed the guy and threw him off his bike. The bike fell over as I jumped on top of him, totally out of control. I wanted to kill the bastard.

All the shop-keepers came running. The old man who ran the tea-stall, eighty-year-old Chachaji, was trying to pull me off.

It took several people to separate us and all I remember afterward was a few friends escorting me home, Rajesh sarcastically saying: "So basically it was a peaceful and blissful time was it?" And when someone told Shyam the next day, he shook his head, looked over at me and simply said: "More purity needed."

Chapter 13

How Was It For You?

All I really wanted to do was ask Shyam where he thought I should go once I returned to Canada. I had no money left. I didn't know whether to return to Vancouver, Gabriola Island or go to Ottawa. Vancouver was more of a familiar home but with some painful memories. I was invited to stay in a Swami Shyam house in Ottawa with people I liked a lot. However, before I was able to ask, Shyam said we should go to the river. So he and three of us meandered on down, had a swim in the cold Beas River and then climbed up to a cave that he knew of.

While sitting in the cave there came upon me a sense I can only describe as grace. It was as though there was no further need for the body and that was perfect. It was as though there was no further need for the mind and that was perfect. There was remaining no hindrance to the freedom I am, no confinement, no thought of a personal nature, no thought at all. While sitting in that cave it was as though the creative intelligence spoke to me, not with words but as plainly as if with words. I heard my name in the silence as though Hansraj was itself the name of that intelligence and I was talking to myself. There was no experience of Samadhi, no Kundalini, no ego receding into itself or dissolving. That was all done. There was none of it, no experience.

We had in fact meditated so deeply in there that Shyam made a point of telling us to be especially careful as we proceeded up the hillside afterward. In spite of that, one fellow slipped and fell. He fell all the way back down to the river, flipped over again and again, eventually landing in a clump of bushes. Had he landed a few feet on either side he would've smashed into the rocks. Shyam called down to some rock-workers nearby to carry him up. Then he said we should go the long way 'round to avoid any further mishap but I protested. "No, come on. We're right there."

Shyam didn't argue and we were in fact back up on the ashram ledge in next to no time. But I was mortified how I'd ordered him like that. He told us to meditate while we waited for the guy who had fallen to be brought up. While I sat with my eyes closed I was consumed by my thoughts. I had ordered Shyam. I had kind of frightened myself by perhaps offending him. After several minutes I opened my eyes and found that Shyam was glaring down at me. I could not meet his gaze until he spoke. "Hansraj." "Yes sir?" "I'm the guru." "Yes sir." And that was all he ever said about it.

He lay down in the meditation room and I kept hankering to ask him whether I should go to Ottawa or Vancouver. Time passed and I wished he would show some signs of life so I could ask; only he was actually snoring. I considered the different ways I could frame my question until out of the blue Shyam rolled over, yawned and looked up at me with faraway eyes. "For God's sake, Hansraj," he said, "just ask."

I became the very first yoga teacher at any public institution or community centre in Ottawa even though I had never done a bit of yoga in my life, ever. When it became clear that I really needed to find work for myself I wandered over to the

Jack Purcell Community Centre and asked if they needed a yoga teacher. It's all I could think of. I was informed that I'd be welcome to put on a demonstration and give a talk about yoga at their upcoming registration evening. Then if enough people signed up I'd be in business. Well I only knew one posture, a yogic headstand, which looks kinda cool. As well, I was a good meditator, a good talker and I was pretty flexible. So I talked, then I did the headstand and, surprisingly, lots of people signed up. My career as a yoga instructor was launched.

Each week before my class one or another of my house-mates would show me a few asana. I would do some reading as well. Then I'd go and teach as though I'd been doing it for years. Because I really knew so little I made the people do postures very slowly with a heck of a lot of meditation in between. After all, I had to fill up an hour and a half. I didn't call it meditation of course. I called it deep relaxation or sivasana, the corpse pose, and they loved it. Sometimes I'd talk during those times, sometimes I'd even chant. My sessions became popular and soon I was teaching yoga at the YM/YWCA as well as condominiums all over the city.

One of my house-mates, Shankar, taught yoga at the house and eventually at the RA Centre near Billings Bridge. He became very proud when the wife of a prominent parliamentarian wanted to come to the house to learn meditation. I don't recall the name of the lady or her esteemed husband but I do recall the morning she came over. She arrived early, while Shankar was in the middle of doing a coffee enema. He used to do that quite often, along with some even more exotic yogic practices, like neti-neti, dhoti and lungi, which I will not describe here. Suffice it to say coffee enemas clean you out pretty drastically but they also tend to leave you pretty drastically wired.

In any event I invited the lady in and left her standing at the base of the stairs while I went up to inform Shankar of her arrival. The bathroom was right at the top of the stairs and I had not gotten halfway back down when Shankar came barreling out. He was clearly out of control. He passed me like 'Northern Dancer' during the 1964 Kentucky Derby. He went to give the lady a hug but was moving so fast that he slammed into her and they both flew out the door and landed in a heap on the front lawn.

My obsession in those days was staying away from women. And to that end I wore a 'langoti' day and night and way too tightly. Basically, a langoti is a traditional Indian undergarment specifically designed for use by scared bramacharis like me. It holds one's lower extremities, one's package so to speak, well in place, under wraps and presumably away from temptation. It's ridiculous of course but I wore mine so tightly that it caused a nasty, nasty rash which got so bad that it eventually required medical attention. When it came time to reveal my rash to the doctor I unraveled the langoti while he watched incredulously, shaking his head in disbelief. In the end he prescribed cortisone cream and told me to hold off wearing underwear altogether for a while. Nothing.

Not even being able to wear underwear of any sort, I was doubly afraid of temptations, of women, of myself really. I was certainly afraid of Denise: tall, beautiful with long, brown hair that she whipped around, an artist with emotional issues that only made her more desirable. She was a little crazy, a little nuts, and I could not stop imagining how incredibly hot it could be. We hung out together a lot. One evening she called to say she absolutely had to see me and although I knew exactly what that meant I agreed. I was definitely ready. I really didn't care anymore. Enlightenment? Self-Realization? Fuggit. I told her to come over in a while, once everyone in the house was asleep.

Meanwhile I also fell asleep while I waited and of course I dreamed of her. I dreamed we were having sex, great sex. It was fantastic. I remember we climaxed in slow motion, together, as I fucked her, most wonderful, full-body, earth-shattering orgasms, shaking and clutching each other tightly as I filled her with spurts of my life-force. That's when I woke up and realized to my horror that I'd had a massive wet-dream. The mattress was absolutely soaked. It was obviously a very full load. I cursed, feeling instantly depressed, dejected, pissed off. And at that very moment Denise called to say she was actually feeling much better but a bit tired and didn't feel like coming over.

That was a devastating and also enlightening moment for me, sitting on the floor after hanging up the phone. Had we just had sex on some alternate level of reality, in some alternate dimension? I felt ripped off, angry, frustrated, upset. I did not like to lose my ojas. None of us did. Of course to have a wet-dream once in a while was quite understandable, especially as a young lad, but I would get upset every time and that time was worse.

Most young yogis have way more wet-dreams than I ever did. It often seemed strange to me that if you wanted the power that comes through abstinence then you really couldn't use it, because then you wouldn't have it. So what the hell is the use of it? Obviously there are many positive and beautiful ways to utilize one's energy other than making oneself shine brightly for women and then having lots of hot sex. I know that now. When you're young and horny, however, you just can't think of any. I must've had some vague idea like that, meanwhile, because I became doubly determined. I kept my head down and stayed the hell away from Denise. Her craziness got worse over the years, eventually had to be institutionalized, heavily medicated and became morbidly obese.

Months went by. I eventually moved to a different house with a few other friends and I was considered a house-leader of sorts. Unfortunately I soon found that place harder than the previous one on a very fundamental level. I was super sensitive to vibrations. If somebody was smoking a joint in the house I could feel it. Without smelling anything the vibrations would roll over me. I would dream other people's dreams. Dope has a specific vibration. Anger has a specific vibration. Sex has a specific vibration. There was no judgment in this knowledge. For me it was just a fact of life. I had trouble meditating and sleeping. I set myself up a private space in the garage with a cot and a chair. The others found it odd and a little insulting I guess but I tried to sit as much as possible in the meditation room in the house and I was usually the last to go to bed.

One night around midnight, while sitting in the meditation room alone, I leaned back against a wall and began to sleep or go into what's called Yog Nidra, a state of deep relaxation, otherwise known as sleep, sort of. The meditation room was under the bedroom of a guy called Natchiketa. At some point while leaning against the wall I began to dream his dream. I don't recall the dream only that it was very sensual, sexual, and I was going all the way. Just at that split second before I was about to ejaculate I sat bolt upright. All that sexual energy shot dramatically straight up within me to the top of my head. At that exact same moment however I heard Natchiketa yell: "Fuck!" Then: "Fuck! Fuck! Fuck!" Then I heard a stomp stomp stomp as he stomped through his room and slammed the bathroom door.

The next morning, while I sat in the kitchen happily eating some granola, Natchiketa came in looking pale and drawn. He had dark circles under his eyes. He was in a bad mood, belligerent. He began to complain that I wasn't doing enough to build up the meditation energy of the house. He complained bitterly about me sleeping in the garage and keeping myself separate. He had a valid point, I thought, as I reached for more granola.

The group dissolved after only a few short months and we all went our separate ways. I tried living in a flat in a downtown house but the curse of being able to feel what was going on all around me in the different flats drove me out. I rented a cabin outside the city. I still continued to teach yoga and held meditation sessions at various places in spite of the long bus rides into town. My sessions were very popular. One young couple who actually met during one of my yoga sessions at the YM/YWCA went on to take meditation from me, ended up getting pregnant and still kept coming. I recall clearly putting my hand on the lady's stomach and saying that because she was a good meditator hers would be a very peaceful child. Twenty years later, back in Ottawa, I bumped into them again purely by chance, along with their two kids: a strapping 18-year-old boy... and a severely mentally disabled 20-year-old daughter who was very very peaceful.

Chapter 14

The Screamer

Before I returned to India again I experimented with the whacky, weird and wonderful world of anal sex, although not with a partner and only once. I wasn't THAT curious. Nevertheless it was mind-blowing, eye-opening and freakish. It was with a candle I met purely by chance, yes, but quite a nice one. It was tall and thick enough but not too thick. It was a tall thick beautiful candle and our short affair was exciting, even explosive, exhilarating, also unsavory, unsettling. I knew it couldn't last. We just weren't meant for each other, I guess, but I don't regret a minute of it.

I don't know about male/female chromosomes or the more scientifically-based understanding of sexual orientations. To me, then, it just seemed as though there was no such thing really as heterosexual or homosexual or bi-sexual. There seemed to be just passion, pure and simple. I felt more fully sexual, definitely, absolutely, than ever. As I've intimated, I found the experience both amazing and confusing.

Dr. Beverly Whipple and Dr. Rajendra Sathe, in their book: 'The G Spot,' write: "In men there is an orgasm triggered by the penis and one triggered by the prostate." Mantak Chia and Douglas Abrams agree and in their book: 'The Multi Orgasmic

Man,' they offer forth rather detailed descriptions of positions and techniques of prostate stimulation for best results. Interestingly, they also add: "The prostate area is a highly erogenous zone, as many men, both gay and straight, have discovered. Many heterosexual men worry that they are gay or will become gay if they enjoy having their anuses stimulated during sex. There is no evidence to suggest a relationship between anal sensitivity and homosexuality. Homosexuality is a sexual orientation, not simply a sexual practice." They warn that it is harder to control the arousal rate with prostate stimulation than genital stimulation, "... so go slowly and try not to push yourself over the edge."

During that time, on one of Shyam's jaunts around Europe and North America, I tagged along, met a lady, Shirley, from Toronto. She was a lovely, wealthy, super hot lady. I have no idea how she came to know of Shyam but she turned up at many of the venues and while Shyam talked endlessly about the all-permeating Self all I could think about was how I wanted to permeate Shirley. I couldn't help it. I knew that once I was back in India I'd be finished and I was scheduled to return very soon.

It was a heady time for me, a welcome respite from what had become a very asexual, unromantic, solitary day-to-day life. I did manage to sneak into Shirley's heart as well as her pants. She took me to fancy Toronto restaurants. Then she'd drag me into a park where we'd roll 'round on the grass. We didn't do 'everything'. I really couldn't and she didn't seem to mind. We did manage an awful lot of grunting, groaning, groping and my balls ached at the end of every night.

My parents meanwhile expressed an interest in meeting Shyam, something I had always dreaded. Shyam however seemed to think it was a fantastic idea and instructed me to bring them next day to the satsang at Glendon campus of York University. In the meantime my sister had come up to Toronto, just to add further stress. She was a member of the Self Realization Fellowship in Mount Washington, California, a very strong personality who clashed with mom on almost all occasions. We meditated together that night but frankly I found it scary. It was long and she meditated as if running a marathon. Peeking at her during that sitting, seeing her ram-rod straight, full-lotus position, red pain-filled face, I was not surprised she still suffered migraines, often. Clearly, nobody had told her meditation is first and foremost a tool for relaxation.

My folks were late arriving next morning. The satsang had already begun, with four-hundred and fifty people in attendance. I had stayed over at the university but apparently there had been a terrible argument between my mom and sister. Mom hadn't wanted to come, dad had a few fast drinks and I met them finally in the parking area. As we approached the hall I was certain my worst fears were about to manifest. My totally dysfunctional hellish family was about to be put on full display for all to see. Upon opening the doors to the hall the whole crowd turned to look at us. Mom shrunk back horrified and refused to go in. I tried to coax her, to no avail. Shyam saw that and did something I will never forget. He got off his tall throne-like seat, climbed off the stage, walked to us, took my mother in his arms and gave her a beautiful hug. Then he led her, along with dad and I, right up to the stage where chairs had been quickly put for us.

What ensued was sure not what I was expecting. It became one of the most wonderful and life-altering sessions personally, ever. Shyam told the story of our first meeting, a couple of hilarious anecdotes from our years together. Then he called a few of my friends to talk about me too. My parents sat dumbfounded in their chairs on the stage. Finally Shyam asked me to give a speech. Sometimes over the years I had made great speeches, terrible speeches, made people laugh or put my foot in my mouth. I'd done it all. But that one, that one mercifully was the best I'd ever given. I had the room and my parents laughing and crying and laughing. And after the session, as I got off the stage, Radha came, wrapped her arms around my neck and said: "You're quite something." I recall her saying it but don't recall responding. I couldn't relate to that, to her. We really hadn't spoken in years. All I could do was stare at her blankly until I was whisked away with my folks for a luncheon with Shyam.

During the lunch Shyam basically ranted at my dad who was totally captivated. My mom meanwhile looked like she wanted to kill a helpless cat, put it in a gunny sack with a brick and toss it into Lake Ontario. There was a long table of people and the proceedings continued to be videoed but Shyam was focused on dad. He was on fire. He hollered the philosophy of oneness and unity to my dad like an evangelist.

I was beside Shyam and at one point he whispered for me to see if my mom could handle a few more minutes. I went 'round the table while dad asked questions and Shyam yelled his responses. I quietly asked mom how she was doing. She barked at me with her gravelly, smoke-ridden voice: **"I have a headache and I need a cigarette!"** I made my way back to my chair beside Shyam and whispered to him: "She's fine." So the session went on for another half-hour.

My parents and I went for dinner later on to a fancy restaurant and that was the first of two times I ever heard my dad make a joke at my mom's expense in front of her. The hostess there asked: "Smokers or non smokers?" And dad responded: "One smoker and two victims." Years later, during their sixtieth wedding anniversary party dad, beginning his speech in front of about a hundred guests, said: "Sixty years. Sixty years. Amazing isn't it? You know, as a judge I can tell you that you'd get out earlier for murder."

Anyway, as opposed to my worst fears the day had turned out to be pretty darn great, one of the most memorable and a turning point in my relationship with the folks. When I returned that night to the university I saw Shyam walking with a group of people out on the lawn. I approached him and began to touch his feet, and he began to stop me as he always did. Then he thought better of it. "Yes," he said. "Tonight I'll let you touch my feet." Once everyone was in their beds I met up with Shirley and we went for a drive. It was a perfect ending to a perfect day.

It may have been some sort of reaction, perhaps a strange act of defiance, that mom decided to cook meat next night for dinner. Normally she at least wouldn't cook red-meat when I was around, which was anyway only once every few years. Still I always appreciated it. But she decided that night was gonna be lamb-chops. Obviously I wasn't expected to eat any and I certainly wouldn't ever say they shouldn't but it just so happened that mom almost immediately began to choke on a piece of her well-cooked dinner.

At first she seemed to just be having a coughing fit. Since mom had smoked since she was about two-and-a-half it was not unusual. Only she began making the most awful noises, like 'aargh aaargh AARGH AARGH' even while coughing, spluttering. Her eyes were bulging. She was panicking. Dad started running all around the kitchen and dining-room yelling:

"I don't know what to do! I don't know what to do!" I just kept sitting there at the table watching. Mom began to half rise up in her chair, turning beet red and clearly suffocating when, for some reason I cannot explain, I slugged her on the back.

I slugged mom really really hard. I slugged her with such force that I scared myself. But everything came rushing out of her. Everything she was choking on and I guess some other stuff too poured out onto the table, and it was incredibly gross. Dad was standing over us staring at the horrendous mess. I looked up at him, grinning stupidly, and said: "Kinda makes you wanna be vegetarian doesn't it?" He apparently did not find my humor appropriate and barked: "That's the great detachment you talk about, that your mother's in trouble and you make jokes?" To which I simply replied: "Hey, who helped her, you or me?"

There was a satsang at the house of an Ottawa devotee a day or two later during which I was seated beside Shyam in a corner of a completely crowded room. It was so full in there that we were all knee over knee, unable to move at all. Shyam ranted on about the Self, the one life permeating all, pure, free, forever. Eventually he suggested everyone meditate a few minutes and he snuck out onto the balcony behind him. I watched him crouch there and wondered if he just needed some air. Everyone filed out at the end of the session. I was last to leave and wandered out onto the balcony. As I stood there looking over the railing I saw Shyam exit the front door. He turned and, at the same moment that I realized I was standing with my bare feet in a puddle of his urine, he waved up to me smiling.

Soon I returned to India but, about six weeks later, Shirley turned up unexpectedly. That was not exactly part of my fantasy.

It was one thing to play around a little in Canada but the ashram was quite a different matter. Suddenly I felt like a total jackass. To welcome her Shyam assembled a bunch of people in a room beside the meditation hall, a lot of us sitting on chairs around the perimeter facing one another. We each had to give a little welcome speech for Shirley. I was about third from the last and during the whole time of waiting and listening I was terrified, flushed and paranoid. Shyam was sitting directly opposite and as I began to squeak out a few words of welcome he wagged his head from side to side, eyes wide, in a most sarcastic fashion as though he was appreciating my speech tremendously.

Shirley and I met a few times during her three-week visit but always in public, at a chai shop or dhaba cafe. In fact, while not wanting to seem rude, I avoided her like the plague. Finally she cornered me the morning of her last day. She was pissed at me and I guess she had good reason to be. So I promised to spend the last evening with her. At the appointed hour I made my way gingerly up the stairs of the house where she was staying. It was a rickety wooden house of a local carpenter, Jagdeesh, his wife, Saraswati, and two little girls.

I had wrapped my langoti super-tightly and yet, in spite of my resolve to keep the evening 'uncomplicated,' we fell onto each other even before dinner. Shirley was wearing some sort of fancy silk designer dress, totally out of place really and yet positively lovely. The certainty of having to give a farewell speech for her in the morning in front of all the people was never far from my thoughts, even after discovering she was not wearing underwear. But I spread her legs and began to eat her like vanilla parfait. We were both naked soon enough; only I still wanted it to be mostly about her.

She tasted delicious; truly a delight that I imagined might never come again. But it went on so long I wondered if she was actually ever gonna cum. She moaned, groaned, grabbed my head. I heard her mutter: "oh my god, oh my god" many times but my neck began to ache; my tongue felt like it was swollen. I soldiered on for what seemed like hours. She was pulling my hair, my fingers felt arthritic. I thought I'd need a neck brace. I really couldn't take much more when all hell broke loose.

All of a sudden Shirley's moans became much deeper, louder, louder, as her body went rigid for a moment before beginning to buck wildly. I held onto her tightly and then she began to scream. She screamed as though her life depended upon it. I had never experienced anything like that before. It was terrific, horrific. It was a primal force of nature. Her screaming was so loud, so intense, that Jagdeesh, Saraswati and, yes, even the kids all came crashing through the flimsy wooden door. They stood at the foot of the bed staring at my naked backside while I straddled Shirley, holding a pillow over her face. Jagdeesh immediately realized what was going on, duh, and pushed his family back, although I did notice Saraswati taking a second look on her way out. Nothing was ever said about the incident. It was never mentioned. Shirley left next day and I never did see her again.

I guess I was about forty-two or forty-three by then. Mahatma Gandhi became celibate at that age. He had been an outspoken critic of artificial birth control and abortion, a stance that was rather unpopular at the time. He believed strongly in the principle of sexual self-control as being personally ennobling and a way toward communion with God, whatever that means. He believed sexual relations should only be between a husband and wife for the purpose of having children. He had a tremendous respect for the life of monks and nuns in various traditions and took a vow of celibacy himself around that time. This he did with his wife's full consent which makes one wonder if he had ever been any good in bed.

Gandhi did have some pretty drastic views on sexuality as well as diet and fasting. He has even been accused of sexual abuse. Apparently he was fond of sleeping with his two young grand-nieces, all naked together regularly. Personally the fact that the girls were so much younger, while kinky enough, does not bother me nearly as much as the fact that they were his grand-nieces. That just feels so wrong, so Ozark-mountain-ish. He was allegedly testing his control, apparently with less than stellar results. Gandhi himself expressed a certain disappointment because he kept getting big erections.

How Would Gandhi's Celibacy Tests Be Viewed Today. By Jan Jack for The Guardian.

Monday, October 1, 2018.

The Indian historian Ramachandra Guha has launched the second volume of his two-volume biography of Mohandas K(Mahatma) Gandhi, a magnificent achievement that, in Guha's words, has taken "30 years of unsystematic interest and 15 years of obsessive foraging". At a talk last week at the London School of Economics, he was passionate and amusing, and it was uplifting to hear his respect and affection for one of the great moral figures of the last century. The questions from the audience mainly concerned Gandhi's role in the independence movement and his attempts to heal India's religious and social divisions. But then – a last question – a young woman wondered about a strange episode in Gandhi's life that she found "unsettling". In reply, Guha went further; it had been "inexplicable and indefensible".

For several decades after his death, this episode was not widely known. Popular accounts of Gandhi's life, including Richard Attenborough's biopic, never mentioned it. The facts are that after his wife, Kasturba, died in 1944, Gandhi began the habit of sharing his bed with naked young women: his personal doctor, Sushila Nayar, and his grandnieces Abha and Manu, who were then in their late teens and about 60 years younger than him.

Gandhi hadn't had a sexual relationship with a woman for 40 years. Nor, in any obvious way and so far as anyone can tell, did he begin one now. His conscious purpose in inviting naked women to share his bed was, paradoxically, to avoid having sex with them. They were there as a temptation: if he wasn't aroused by their presence, he could be reassured he'd achieved brahmacharya, a Hindu concept of celibate self-control. According to Gandhi, a person who had such control was "one who never has any lustful intention, who by constant attendance upon God has become proof against conscious or unconscious emissions, who is capable of lying naked with naked women, however beautiful they may be, without being in any manner sexually excited". Such a person, Gandhi wrote, would be incapable of lying or harming anyone.

Why was this so important to Gandhi at that time? Because he believed – fantastically, egotistically – that the Hindu-Muslim violence then sweeping India had some connection to his own failings. He had come round to the view, as Guha writes, "that the violence around him was in part a product or consequence of the imperfections within him". And those imperfections, which he scrupulously recorded and publicised, included the "nocturnal emissions" (wet dreams) that had occurred in the years 1924, 1936 and 1938 to spoil a record of celibate living that began in South Africa in 1906, and which led each time to bouts of self-disgust.

He believed sex existed only to procreate and never to enjoy, a view that his political ally Jawaharlal Nehru found "unnatural and shocking". Lust was the enemy; that lesson was learned when, as a married 16-year-old, he had left his sick father's bedside to be with his wife and, as they made love, his father had died. As to any unconscious motivation for bed-sharing, who knows? As one of the world's most famous men, a magnetic celebrity, he rarely hesitated to exploit his attraction to women in order to benefit from the help and care they offered. In his ashram, the psychoanalyst Sudhir Kakar has written: "The competition among women for Gandhi's attention was as fierce as it is in any guru's establishment today."

His behaviour in the winter of 1946-47 shocked many of his followers. At least two of his helpers, his stenographer and his Bengali translator, quit his service in protest when they discovered that he was sleeping with 19-year-old Manu. The Indian press stayed silent. Unusually, Gandhi kept his "experiment" with Manu reasonably private – behaviour that he later regretted because it violated the principle that the seeker after truth must keep nothing hidden.

No evidence suggests the young women themselves bore Gandhi any ill will. Manu and Abha were walking at either side of him – they were known as his "walking sticks" – when his assassin ran forward with a pistol in a Delhi garden in January 1948, a year after he brought his experiments in celibate sexuality to a close.

The fond name for Gandhi was Bapu, meaning father, but a short memoir that Manu wrote later is titled Bapu – My Mother, a contradictory phrase that at first sight is an odd way to describe a man who has used you as a test of his desire. In fact, her mother had died when she was a child. Gandhi's wife had adopted her and, when she died in turn, Gandhi assumed the maternal role. He cooked and cared for her, and Manu noted in her diary that his conversation "was filled with affection greater than any mother could feel". But there was more than simple familial duty at work here. Gandhi often liked to say he was half a woman: in the words of another historian, Vinay Lal, "it is almost plausible to speak of Gandhi's vulva envy". He liked to play with sexual boundaries. In this, as in his environmentalism, his diet and his techniques of protest, he prefigured our age.

To dislocate phenomena from the present to the past is usually pointless. Does anyone care how Shakespeare would have voted in the EU referendum? Nonetheless, it's interesting to consider how our present moral temperament would have reacted to the news of Gandhi's experiments. A powerful old man, subordinate young women, nudity: he would surely have been widely reviled, and his faults distorted and oversimplified in the rush to judge him. A blot on his reputation would have become enormously magnified – a sad end to a humane and world-changing life.

In this circumstance, George Orwell might never have written the epitaph that Guha repeats in his final pages – the fact that: "Compared with the other leading political figures of our time, how clean a smell he has managed to leave behind!"

Sigmund Freud felt that sexual activity was incompatible with the accomplishing of any great work. According to his biographer, Ernest Jones, Freud became strictly celibate from the age of forty until his death "...in order to sublimate the libido for creative purposes." Nietzsche, Michelangelo, Newton, Pythagoras, Plato, Aristotle, Spinoza, Kant and Beethoven are some other famous names bandied about as philosophers, artists and scientists who preferred to sublimate the sex drive so as to increase their creativity and concentrate their energy.

My aunt Doris was celibate for a long time, not by choice or for any religious, creative or intellectual reason. She simply couldn't find a boyfriend. I once told approximately one-hundred-and-fifty people about it. Shyam called me up to give a speech, as he often did. But this time he specifically asked me to talk about relationships. Many in the audience began to chuckle. They knew how ridiculous Hansraj trying to sound like he knew much of anything on that subject could be. But I got an idea. I talked about how my aunt Doris tried and tried to find a boyfriend and eventually succeeded. Aunt Doris and all the family members, I continued, were very happy then. After a long while and a lot of hoping and praying, aunty finally got engaged. She and the family were again all very happy.

Following the wedding, so the story went, there was a long period of hoping for a child. I told the crowd how much anguish the whole family felt at my aunt and her husband's seemingly futile attempts to produce any offspring. I stretched that part of the story out as I built to a climax, excuse the expression. My aunt finally finally became pregnant and everyone was so incredibly happy then. And after nine months the joyous occasion arrived. She gave birth. The only problem was that the newborn child, I said, was ninety percent retarded.

At that point in my speech I realized it was not the least bit funny or even amusing. The look of horror on people's faces told me just how un-funny I was being. I had said 'retarded' rather than the more politically correct term, 'mentally challenged,' thinking it funnier. But really nothing could've been further from the truth. The crowd was stunned, shocked, silent.

Still I believed I could salvage the situation by making my point: that no matter how much we hanker for something, desire and plan for something, we are not in total control of our own destinies. I thought I could still make the point but, before I could continue, Shyam leaned over close to the microphone and said: "Are you sure that wasn't your mother?" The crowd went wild. The roof practically flew off the hall as everyone howled with laughter and I died a horrible death. As the laughter continued I slunk off the stage and onto my cushion near the middle of the room. People clapped me on my back and jostled me as I hung my head.

Back in my cabin I packed my bags. I wanted to leave. I was finished, done, very definite. I only had to wait for the evening bus. In the meantime I went for a walk and somehow ended up at the ashram. As I wandered through the gates I was surprised to hear Shyam's voice. He called out to me from up in a tree. "Hi Hansraj. How are you?" "I'm upset," I responded. "Upset?" "Because of my speech." Then Shyam said something that somehow totally changed my outlook. "Why?," he asked incredulously. "I thought we did very well." It was the word 'we' that changed everything. In that moment I realized that if it's 'we' instead of 'me' then the speech was indeed fantastic. "Come on, Hansraj," he cajoled. "Come on up and help me prune these trees." So instead of leaving India forever I spent a nice afternoon pruning trees with my guru.

I was with Shyam in those days a lot playing chess, over-seeing building projects, as a kind of messenger or for many other reasons. However, it began to change and one day in satsang he said: "Hansraj's mind wants to be close to me doing all sorts of jobs but his space just wants to be free. I'm not going to listen to his mind anymore." That was kind of tough for me. On another occasion he even said that I wasn't really his type. To that I petulantly remarked: "If you're not my guru maybe you should just let me know." To which he responded: "It's not a matter of whether I'm your guru or not. I am guru." I was not happy about the change, for quite a while. Yet as time went on I realized that he was right. I really liked just being free to play basketball, walk in the hills, do my business, and live my life. As well, as more time went along I came to understand that I was actually not his type. I understood it needn't minimize the love and affection. It just was what it was.

I began my business initially in gems. So I'd of course trundle off on periodic buying trips to the major lapidary centers such as Agra or Jaipur. And in those early days I was not very sophisticated in how I went about it. That could cause problems, like the time I forgot my passport.

Since the assassination of Indira Gandhi in 1984 the official attitude toward foreigners had changed. Canada was accused of harboring Sikh Kalhistani separatists. Hotels were being watched more carefully, passport information and visas were fundamental. Aside from forgetting my passport I didn't have enough bank receipts to cover the amount of rupees I was carrying; and I was also carrying far too much jewelry in my bag. I was a mess. I filled in all the spaces of the register at the hotel as closely as I could recall but I left the space for visa number blank. That was really dumb. Had I written any number at all I'd have probably been all right. The police however saw that I was Canadian, had no visa number: I was in trouble. The hotel was in trouble.

Returning to the hotel that hot afternoon with a large case full of money and jewelry and no proper papers whatsoever, I encountered a lobby full of freaked-out hotel people and onlookers. The police had been there. I tried to get them to let me fill in the blank but it was far too late for that. They insisted I accompany them down to the police station. It occurred to me that trotting off to see the local gendarme would probably mean the end of my business if not my stay in India, not to mention my personal freedom.

While these unsettling thoughts flitted through my mind the crowd grew and the situation deteriorated. The hoteliers became progressively more frantic, loud and aggressive. Since I'd never stayed there before, I didn't know anyone at all. At one point the manager grabbed my arm; I pulled it away and may have said something uncomplimentary about his mother. He grabbed me again, harder. Then I lost my composure. I panicked. I pushed him into the crowd and ran like hell, lugging my heavy case along. Ignoring the 42-degree scorching heat I tore through the streets with at least four men on my heels. They were yelling but of course I dared not look 'round. Twisting and turning through the thick market I ran like the devil until I made yet another mistake. I ran straight into a dead-end alley. I was trapped. I looked around wildly for any way out, a place to run, somewhere to hide.

Then a remarkable thing happened. An old lady, dressed in the meanest of rags, whistled to me. She motioned for me to crawl in to a kind of small garage in amongst tires and old cans. Once inside, some children, as unclean and unkempt as the lady, threw jute bags on top of me before continuing on with their games as though nothing unusual was happening. The old lady swept around the entrance and as the men ran up to the lane I actually saw her pointing onward. After a few long minutes the children uncovered me and helped shove me over a stone and mud wall. I swallowed some dirt as I clawed my way over and dropped down into what appeared to be an entirely new market. I hopped into a scooter, choking, coughing, gasping for air and told the driver to head for Gangotri Bazaar. I had escaped. I could hardly believe what had happened in that alley and I never thanked the lady or those kids.

Having narrowly escaped an Indian lynch-mob and the Indian penal system, for the moment, I took the scooter to the home of a business acquaintance and hunkered down for the next couple days. My host and his family took good care of me. They spared no effort to make me comfortable, help me to feel at home and reassure me that all would be right in the end. Of course I was dropping nearly fifty thousand rupees into the family coffers through my purchases but I like to think they really cared.

After completing our business, we ate a meal to celebrate and then my friend and his family sent me on my way happily. I mean they sent me happily on my way. The huge crowd at the Interstate Bus Terminal, however, made it impossible for me to get to the wicket counter until a man with an impressive handlebar moustache took an interest in helping. As the friendly fellow ran interference for me I managed to claw my way to the counter and acquire a ticket and I thanked him profusely for the help.

Still somewhat paranoid, I moved to the opposite side of the street to watch the loading of the bus from a safe distance. And as I watched from a doorway across the road I saw that same man with the handlebar moustache ride up on a police jeep. With several officers hanging off the vehicle, fingering their holsters and swinging their big sticks, he was pointing excitedly to the bus for New Delhi.

My lower extremities dissolved. The scene in front of me unfolded as if in slow motion. As the police began searching the bus, the driver's registry and the surrounding area, I slid to the ground and slithered away. I beat another hasty retreat through another alley to another street, jumped into another rickshaw and scooted back to the same old house of my business friend. They appeared somewhat less than enthusiastic to see me so soon again. Still they let me in, quickly closed the door and, not into reminiscing about the good old days, spirited me out of town soon after dusk. I was dropped off unceremoniously at the side of a dark highway to catch local busses all the way to New Delhi. But I was free. The matter never came up again, well, except once.

After that particular ill-fated trip to 'The Pink City' I sorely regretted having to leave behind a certain pair of jeans in the hotel. I had been rather attached to those trousers. They were western, fit like a glove, beautifully faded, even had patches on the knees and they were Levis. Yeah, clearly I'd been in India a long time.

I returned to Jaipur on business a couple of months later. Devi was with me that time and I felt sure there wouldn't be any trouble. I had all my documents and I couldn't resist. I devised a bold, brave and gallant plan. We'd take a scooter to the hotel, Devi would enter and demand her boyfriend's lost Levi pants. I would keep a watch from the safety of our scooter. So not in fact very brave or gallant. And as it turned out I saw my plan unravel horribly as more and more people gathered. I even saw one of the hotel workers slip away and run, obviously toward the police station.

Needless to say, aside from not getting the pants, we were fortunate to get away with our shorts. As Devi jumped aboard the scooter in a near panic, disillusioned with my plan and perhaps with me, the men began to move ominously toward us. They were collectively frowning, except for one boy standing off to the side who was actually smiling. And as I looked back through the little plastic rear window I realized why. He was wearing my pants.

I often fantasized about meeting a lady on one of those business trips, having a one-nighter, a hot fling. I always wondered what I'd do if faced with the possibility, if I actually met someone. Well, she turned out to be a striking, dark-haired beauty, a bit sleazy-looking, a bit tough-looking but with a killer body. We chatted in the lobby of the guest-house, since we were checking in at the same time, and I bumped into her again on Janpath Avenue shortly afterward.

My imagination really went into overdrive when she looked back at me and smiled while walking away. I fell asleep in the early evening but was awoken around ten-thirty. I don't recall what woke me up but there was a bright light on in the adjoining room. I could see in quite easily through the old semi-opaque glass doors that weren't even closed all the way. Lying on the bed was a girl, that girl, and she was as naked as the day she was born, only bigger. She was smoking a cigarette, drinking a beer, leafing through a magazine and just seemed to be waiting for me to walk in. It was as if she was saying: 'I know you've been fantasizing about me for a long long time honey. Well here I am. Are you ready? Are you man enough to do it?' Of course she may have simply been contemplating her next day travel plan.

In any event I kept the light off. My heart was pounding as I sat on my bed, then walked to the door, retreated to my bed, then went back to the door. I knew that all I needed to do was knock, ask for a cigarette. She'd offer me a warm beer as well and we'd be off and running like a couple of Greyhounds. Was I barking mad? It was irrelevant that I didn't smoke, didn't drink, even that I was a tremendously strict bramachari yogi. I was a healthy guy, it hadn't rained in a long long time and my fantasy was right there. I decided that I was in fact man enough. I purposefully walked to the door and was about to flick on my light-switch when I noticed movement from her room. She was getting up. She put out her cigarette, stepped off the bed, walked over to the dresser to get something from on top and, man oh man, she was hideous.

Without her bra and her tight jeans to hold everything in place, without her makeup, her hair-clips or her shoes with heels, she was unbelievably ugly. The years of hard living and decadence showed up in every aspect of her face, her body, and I shuddered involuntarily as I scuttled back to my bed. I was still shuddering as it occurred to me that I had barely dodged a bullet. There was a lesson in that. There was a tremendous moral. I just couldn't figure it out right at that moment.

Chapter 15

Just Keep Thinking About It

In her book, 'How To Be Alone,' Scottish author, Sarah Maitland, writes: "I got fascinated by silence, by what happens to the human spirit, to identity and personality when the talking stops, when you press the off button, when you venture out into that enormous emptiness. I was interested in silence as a lost cultural phenomenon, as a thing of beauty and as a space that had been explored and used over and over again by different individuals, for different reasons and with wildly differing results. I began to use my own life as a sort of laboratory to test some ideas and to find out what it felt like. Almost to my surprise, I found I loved silence. It suited me. I got greedy for more.

"We have arrived," Maitland continues, "in the relatively prosperous developed world, at a cultural moment which values autonomy, personal freedom, fulfillment and human rights, and above all individualism, more highly than they have ever been valued before in human history. At the same time these autonomous, free, self-fulfilling individuals are terrified of being alone."

Obviously I was no stranger to silence, to being alone, no stranger to myself. Meditation, Samadhi, was everything to me, almost. It did often occur to me that a subtle, not so subtle, rather persistent desire for a relationship lingered. And I had occasion to get Shyam's opinion about that during what had become a rare private moment with him. I started by acknowledging the fact that I had been meditating for over twenty years by then. In fact I had been meditating more exclusively and with more dedication than most people in that or any other ashram, monastery or cave. So I suggested that, since I still thought about the sensual life, the family life, after all those years, perhaps I should just go and get it out of my system. Shyam laughed, said I was wrong, that it wouldn't work like that. He said it would only make me more full of desire and at the same time bound up with wife and kids for twenty years.

So I asked what he would suggest in that case. He looked at me closely, smiled and said: "Better you just keep thinking about it." When I asked about all the couples at the ashram he remarked that it was fine but that they were: "not really doing the trip." That felt so strange. I was very aware that he often said totally different things to different folks and that may have been perfect for me. At the same time, as I sat in a chai shop after our meeting, I knew beyond any doubt and definitely not for the first time that I wasn't actually 'on a trip' anymore. Any idea of seeking or striving for enlightenment was over for me. It's not as if I decided I was enlightened, self-realized and fully free. Not at all. I hoped that if there was more to attain that it would somehow miraculously happen but I realized I really was done.

Shyam's opinion seemed curious to me also considering he had a wife and five children. Baba Hari Das, a silent monk his whole life, used to often suggest marriage for his disciples. Goenka was a married man with no children. He refused to voice an opinion other than to say meditation was a must in either case. None of the great eastern masters of my time ever really lived alone.

They were constantly surrounded by devotees, tended to and doted on by people all the time. Sometimes it felt as though I was the only yogi truly alone. Of course there may have been many great sadhus in Himalayan caves leading solitary lives, coming out only for the Maha Kumbh Mela after each twelve year period. I knew that to be true, had even met a few. What about the Lamas of Tibet, past and present, the monks and nuns in monasteries and convents around the world?

In his book, 'The Notebook,' acclaimed novelist, screenwriter and producer Nicholas Sparks wrote: "We sit silently and watch the world around us. This has taken a lifetime to learn. It seems only the old are able to sit next to one another and not say anything and still feel content. The young, brash and impatient, must always break the silence. It is a waste, for silence is pure. Silence is holy. It draws people together because only those who are comfortable with each other can sit without speaking. This is the great paradox."

Baba Hari Das, to use his example again, is an Indian monk who has not spoken since 1952 and has lived in the west since 1970. Known simply as Babaji, he founded the Mount Madonna Centre in Santa Cruz, California. He writes on a small blackboard hanging around his neck. In his book, 'Silence Speaks,' it is recorded that when asked what his greatest pleasure is, Babaji wrote: 'silence.' I did have the pleasure of being with Babaji several times in the '70s and will always remember the waves of 'saktipad,' peace, that rolled over me virtually every time we sat together.

Nelson Mandela was once quoted as saying: "It is never my custom to use words lightly. If twenty-seven years in prison have done anything for me, it was to use the silence of solitude to make me understand how precious words are and how real speech is in its impact on the way people live and die."

Meanwhile one of my more lucrative side-businesses in those early days of my business was changing U.S. dollars on the black market. It was just a wee bit illegal. Of course it can't be just a wee bit illegal. The thing is either legal or illegal and that thing was illegal. It was most definitely against the laws of the land and pretty tricky. Folks at the ashram would hand over their foreign currency; I'd change it all while on one of my business trips and keep half of the profit for my trouble, not to mention the very real risks involved. As well, many of my customers would pay me for the gems and gifts they purchased with foreign currency.

On one occasion during a busy day in New Delhi, I realized I had lost my shoulder-bag. Having also been in the gold and silver market that day in Chandni-Chowk, the bag not only had thousands of dollars in it, along with about one-hundred thousand rupees without bank receipts, it was full of gems and jewelry and, oh yeah, my passport too. So once again I was basically screwed, completely and utterly screwed.

In my mind there was no doubt I'd left the bag in the last scooter-rickshaw I had been in. But trying to find it would've been like looking for the proverbial needle in a haystack and I knew it. I tried of course. Eventually, however, close to tears, I retreated to my usual room at the Gandhi Guest House, sat down on the bed and put my head in my hands.

Perhaps as a last resort or out of desperation I just decided to be still, to be silent. It wasn't meditation exactly, at least not formally. I was just sitting and I kept on sitting for quite a while. I didn't often feel as though meditation while on those trips was really very good. One should not label any sitting as good or less good but that's how I felt. Still, that one, while just sitting and not meditating, took me somewhere special. I had been to the place before, like a room at the bottom under the waves. I was conscious, alert but I had no problem, no bag was missing, my life as I knew it was not ending because it had not begun. Perhaps I'd given up hope and there was a subtle blissful freedom in that.

Then strangely, from out of that space or place, a thought occurred to me. I recalled briefly being at the 'Western Union' office in the 'Imperial Hotel.' My next thought was that I had my bag after that. Nevertheless I slid off my bed and shuffled listlessly down the street to the hotel. As I walked into the 'Western Union' office there was a large crowd around a bag, my bag, all staring down at it. I immediately was so relieved and immediately realized that they thought it might be a bomb. That was clear, although then you gotta wonder why they were crowding around it. I also realized the police would descend upon the scene within another few moments. So I wound my way through the crowd, grabbed the bag and quickly left the building. I was elated, thanked the creative intelligence, my lucky stars and every deity I could think of for that one thought which came from out of silence.

In 'Reflections on Talks with Sri Ramana Maharshi', it is reported that he said: "Silence and solitude is in the mind. One may be in the thick of the world and maintain serenity of mind. Such a one is in solitude. Another may be in a forest, but still unable to control his or her mind. That one cannot be said to be in solitude. One attached to desire cannot get solitude wherever he or she may be. A detached person is always in solitude."

Chapter 16

Doin It Doggy Style

Mayama had a reputation as a great masseuse. I didn't have any great desire for massages but I did have a great desire to fondle her bountifully big beautiful breasts. Looking back now I can hardly say I'm proud of it but I engaged her services and things went along pretty much as I'd hoped. She'd do her thing, I'd act like an idiot and we were having fun. Only every time it got a little steamy Mayama had the strange habit of suddenly sitting up ram-rod straight, crossing her legs and beginning to meditate. If it weren't so frustrating I might've even found it inspiring. She would meditate while I lay beside her, waiting. Eventually the whole procedure would begin again. We would never get beyond a certain point before she'd sit up and assume the position. We met a few times and I'm not sure why she even returned but eventually we stopped. I didn't ask for massages, she didn't ask why. We just stopped.

Meanwhile I walked into the hall one evening right around that time and spotted a beautiful girl I'd never seen before. She was sitting with eyes closed and in the candlelight she looked like an angel. I said to myself: 'I gotta meet that one.' Spotting her in a café alone the very next day I slipped into a seat nearby, struck up a conversation and the rest is history.

Jaya had a ready laugh, a lovely smile. We began to hang out together. Neither of us wanted to bring much attention to that fact. She was a very beautiful, elegant and, most importantly, a new girl in town. As well, I was considered to be in a relationship with Devi. At the ashram it didn't matter that Devi and I did not have a sexual relationship. We were considered a couple. I always tried to call her my sister. She always tried to call me her husband, and that's just the way it was.

I quickly realized I was out of my depth with Jaya. She was a lady who generally got what she wanted, especially when it came to men. And she did not exactly understand or appreciate my ambivalence toward normal sexual relations. Bramacharya was a foreign and unacceptable concept to her. We swiftly went from casual conversation at a café to secretly sleeping together most nights. We would sneak into a room at the local hotel, snuggle up on a bed and watch videos in the afternoons. We'd drive to other valleys just to spend time together.

On one of those hot afternoons I nearly drove us off a cliff. I understood almost too late how hard it is to stay focused on the driving when a beautiful lady had her mouth all over my dick. On another of those hot afternoons Jaya was bent over my bed and I was banging her hard from behind when Devi all of a sudden began banging my front door hard from behind. Her pounding was so violent that I thought the door might fly off its hinges and we both freaked. I called out that I was meditating. Jaya actually slid under the bed. Devi kept on banging the door. It was a classic situation. We assumed Devi must've discovered the horrible truth but, when I finally flung the door open, Devi began hollering something about her dog Ralph choking to death somewhere down on the road.

The next thing I knew I was running with Devi down the hill, buttoning my shirt on the fly. When we got to the road a rather large crowd had surrounded the dog that was in fact choking, convulsing in the dirt. For some reason and with no thought I ran straight through the group, grabbed up Ralph roughly and began applying the Heimlich maneuver. I really didn't know what the hell I was doing. I was on automatic. Basically I was demonstrating what I had been doing with Jaya in my cabin hardly a few minutes earlier. There really was visually not much difference. The strangest part was that it worked. Ralph projectile vomited and everyone began clapping. I dropped the mutt, took a theatrical bow and quickly made my way back home. Of course Jaya was long gone.

It hardly took a couple of weeks, however, before the 'fit did hit the shan' so to speak. Jaya was far too pretty, way too sexy and she'd stolen one of the ashram men. It'd be fair to say that Devi's personality, normally loving, warm and giving, could would and did undergo a surprisingly drastic change. The wonderful drama played out in peoples' homes, in cafes, on street corners and even in the meditation hall. I was responsible of course but it was Jaya who got the brunt of the abuse. We still spent most nights in each other's arms, still snuck away in the afternoons. I never actually released the hounds, so to speak, although nobody would've believed it or cared.

At the height of the drama I met up with Shyam by chance one early morning and we talked. He had told a fellow, Shruti, who had been in somewhat similar circumstances about a year earlier, to be strictly celibate. He was to strictly view each girl as a mother, daughter or sister. That was Shyam's recipe for Shruti to extricate himself from the situation he was in. So I asked Shyam if I shouldn't just do the same, make it known and be done with the whole 'affair.' He refused but he did offer two suggestions: 1. "You need to live in this world while not being of the world. And: 2. "You need to live a little less for yourself and a little more for other people."

Jaya left for England soon enough. We kept in contact at first. I'd call her from the only phone, which happened to be in the local tailor shop. The problem was Jaya apparently liked phone sex and that was a wee bit uncomfortable for me. It's hard to really get into the mood with a bunch of tailors sitting a few feet away even if their English wasn't too good. To those guys the conversation probably sounded a bit like: "Oh yeah, that'd be great. Yeah, I'd like that. Sure. Uhuh, go ahead, that's nice. We should..." Needless to say the long-distance relationship didn't really work out.

And then came the AIDS scare. By the early '90s AIDS had become the leading cause of death for all Americans aged twenty-five to forty-four. As well, it had spread around the world. In 1986 the first known case was diagnosed amongst female sex workers in Chennai. Foreigners traveling in and out of India were blamed. In 1992 the government set up the National AIDS Control Organization to try and control its spread. To those of us ex-pats living at the ashram it meant that we were compelled to have blood-tests done.

Although nobody liked it the tests were not so bad. We each trundled off to the local chemist shop to buy a disposable needle, went to the hospital, gave the blood and went on home for dinner. If you didn't buy a needle of course there was a real concern because of the less than exemplary hygiene at the local hospital but nobody in their right mind would put themselves in that position. It was all good, until one test came back positive.

My very good friend Rajesh, unfortunately, apparently had AIDS. My good friend Rajesh, unfortunately, also was one of the very few sexually active people at the ashram. Not only had he slept with two or four ladies over those years there, I happened to know he had frequented a couple of whore-houses in other parts of India. In fact he had even boasted to me once that sex was so cheap in India that it really didn't make sense to masturbate. In any event it was entirely plausible that he could've contracted the disease.

Rajesh was immediately put under house arrest and a police guard was placed outside his door. He was allowed visitors but no leaving the premises and presumably no sex. During the time it took to get results from a second test Rajesh and I, along with a few others, drew up graphs showing who else might have become infected if he had AIDS. It became a surprisingly complex graph. There were a lot of pretty worried people walking around pretending to be entirely unconcerned. Rajesh died a thousand deaths during those days but he was not dying of AIDS. He was eventually cleared and life went back to normal, sort of.

I never had any inclination to follow Rajesh's wonderful example of sampling Indian whore-houses, at all. However, a strip-joint in Jaipur on a business trip caught my eye. It was called: 'The Jaipur Ice Cream Club' and I stood in front of that place for a long time looking at a picture of a fluffy lady called Mojoini. Eventually I went in, paid a few rupees and passed through a faded red curtain into a brightly-lit, hazy room with a lot of men smoking and drinking and talking but no women. Not one woman. There were no women stripping or otherwise. Eventually, however, I noticed men going down and coming up some stairs near the back. It led down into a kind of dark, dank, dirty dungeon, thick with more smoke, music blaring but nobody was talking. The men sat quietly at round tables watching intently. At the front was a stage with a broken disco ball over it and a slightly over-weight lady dancing to a Bollywood film song.

Madam Mojoini was the worst dancer I'd ever seen and not an exotic dancer at all. She did take her shirt off but there was a shirt underneath. Her under-shirt was a kind of cut-off tank-top. She clearly had a bra under that. And anyway she kept putting her red and black over-shirt back on, then taking it off, then putting it on again. She had a long red skirt replete with sequins. Her eyes were darkened by cadjul. Her hair was long, black and she would whip it around somewhat in pace with the music as she sashayed around the stage. I ordered a 'Kingfisher' beer, pretended to sip it, sat back and wondered why I'd come.

Mojoini's dancing was a type of hybrid belly-free-form-jazz-affair. It wasn't particularly sensual. It wasn't particularly anything. Nevertheless she held the attention of each and every man as she built up to some sort of climax, moving faster and faster. All eyes were on her as she took off her shirt and put it back on coquettishly again and again. All eyes were on the way she repeatedly thrust out her hips as though she either needed a hip replacement or would soon need a hip replacement. Clearly the attraction had everything to do with it being not the way ladies acted in normal Indian society. And there were, after all, bare shoulders and midriff from time to time.

The actual climax, I supposed, came when the lady stepped off the stage. She began wandering around the room shaking every man's hand. As the music continued to blare Mojoini went from table to table, from chair to chair shaking every man's hand.

She made a point of 'connecting' with each man with a hand-shake and a smile but she missed me. She missed only me. Out of the whole friggin room-full of captivated, wide-eyed, excited, sweaty men of all shapes and sizes, mine was the only hand undefiled, a fact I found somehow strangely significant.

Back at the ashram my dog Missy went into 'heat'. She and her 'significant other' were perfect examples of a little-understood phenomenon euphemistically called 'chemistry'. Missy was a particularly large shaggy dog who used to go everywhere with me. Many of the local folks were scared of her simply because of her size, although she was really very gentle. Missy had been spayed but unfortunately she could still go into heat. The vet botched the operation. She couldn't have puppies but about three times a year she would cause quite a ruckus in the neighbourhood. It may not have been the vet's fault exactly since the power went out right in the middle of the procedure. The lights of course went off regularly for hours and even days at a time. We should've been better prepared for that eventuality. As it was I had to hold up a flashlight while he continued but the vet really couldn't see what he was doing.

When Missy would go into heat the local dogs would all go nuts trying to get at her. She was safe in my courtyard although we could hear the horrible fighting going on right outside. They would be berserk with desire. I could see paws reaching in under the door as if trying in desperation to grab her. When I took Missy for walks at that time she was quite happy for me to put her on a leash and I carried a big stick to beat off the other dogs. We would often jump in a scooter-rickshaw and speed to a different valley, to get away from the pack, until another pack would begin to form.

Missy was completely uninterested in having intimate relations with any of the dogs in the area. She really was not the least attracted to any... except one. I came to know eventually that Missy was terribly in love with one and only one of those carnivorous canine creatures. She had a fancy for the smallest, scrawniest of the lot. She liked the one that was kind of a mix between a Chihuahua and a gerbil. For some reason Missy always played with that dog, liked to hang out with that one and, when in heat, she would cry for only him.

What could I do? I loved Missy and Missy loved that little creature. So I arranged for the two of them to spend some quality time together even while Missy was in her hotness. The three of us would jump in a scooter-rickshaw. Missy would keep her partner under some control by virtue of her more commanding size until we reached the next valley. It was not always a particularly comfortable drive for me but once we got out of the vehicle I just let them be free to work out the logistics themselves, which always amazed me. They would find a small hill, Missy would back up to it while her under-sized partner went up onto it and that's how they consummated their love.

There's a rather well-known painting created by a famous painter named Shobha Singh. It depicts a lovely girl wearing a simple sari and shawl and holding a water jug. A handsome boy has an arm around her waist while the two run against the wind. Their expressions are as if they're either in love or in distress, which of course can seem quite similar.

The story behind the painting is of the girl who was from a wealthy Sikh family, and the boy who was a poor Hindu. They lived on opposite sides of a large lake and although they were deeply in love their families were against the match. In fact eventually they were forbidden to meet. They'd gaze over at each other from opposite shores and in the end couldn't stand to stay apart. The boy began swimming toward the girl but it was too far and he floundered. Seeing the boy in trouble the girl swam out to him and they both drowned together in the middle of the lake.

They were in love. And that love transcended all differences. In fact they wanted to be together so much that they were willing to die rather than stay apart.

The Lebanese poet Kahlil Gibran of the early nineteen hundreds wrote; 'Love one another but make not a bond of love; let it rather be a moving sea between the shores of your souls.' I rather prefer what the fifteenth-century poet Kabir wrote about love. Born Hindu, raised as a Muslim, Kabir became a weaver and spun not only cloth but yarns that have endured through the ages. In one of his most famous love poems he wrote; 'you can't live with them and you can't live with them.' Ok that may not have been one of his. He wrote; 'Why should we two ever want to part? This love between us goes back to the first humans. It cannot be annihilated. Here is Kabir's idea: As the river gives itself to the ocean, I give myself to you.'

True love transcends race, creed and colour, even species. 'Inside her water jug there are canyons and pine-mountains,' Kabir wrote. 'And the maker of canyons and mountains. All seven oceans are inside and hundreds of millions of stars. The acid that tests gold, the one who judges jewels and the music from the strings no one touches and the source of all water. If you want the truth, I will tell you, friend. Listen. God and the one I love are inside.'

There had been plenty of chemistry of course between Jaya and me. And nearly two years later when she returned to Kullu all hell broke loose yet again, although not right away. She actually didn't want anything to do with me at first. No time had elapsed in my mind as I was consumed by pent-up desire. She was as beautiful as ever and I couldn't understand how she could be so aloof. It really drove me nuts. I began to resemble a local dog chasing Missy. But a couple of years had in fact elapsed for Jaya during which I hadn't contacted her, not since those early phone calls, not even when I passed through London one time. She'd been working hard while continuing to raise her daughter alone. So when she planned another short visit to Kullu her family impressed upon her the need to stay away from that asshole who ruined her last visit.

Still it only took a few days for me, the asshole, to break through Jaya's defenses. She finally let me into her room one evening but just to talk. She sat on the bed. I was instructed to sit in the chair. We talked and at one point she said something about weeds having grown over her heart and I responded: "Oh well if it's just a matter of a little weeding I can do that." She laughed, I jumped on her bed and we spent the night wrapped up in each other's arms. It felt totally right and natural. Her feel, her scent, her taste were as familiar to me as family. It was undeniable. Jaya however was adamant that I was not allowed to have intercourse with her and I was to leave before daylight. She said she'd 'fuck my brains out' if I went to London with her but not otherwise. I did as I was told, happy and content.

For me to be found walking along the road as the light of day first began to show itself was nothing new. So when Ravi, out for an early morning stroll himself, met me there he thought nothing of it. He began to tell me about a meeting with Shyam from the previous night. Apparently, with a bunch of people in his room, including Devi, he all of a sudden stopped talking, paused a moment and then announced that Hansraj and Jaya were back together again. Ravi said everyone howled with laughter. They assumed he was just teasing Devi. Of course I laughed too while he told me the story, then slunk on home with my tail tucked tightly between my legs.

We carefully kept our affair a secret for about ten days until Jaya fell ill. She actually passed out on the street right in front of the ashram one intensely hot Himalayan afternoon and as people leaned over to help she began asking for me. The cat was effectively out of the bag. I was called, a few of us carried her to my place which was close to the ashram in those days, and there she stayed for a couple of nights. The fit hit the shan once again. Be that as it may Jaya remained definite about not having actual intercourse with me unless I followed her to London that time, which of course I did. I was frustrated. At that point I woulda gone to Nunavat.

For the very first time since living with Radha in Vancouver more than twenty years earlier, I shared a bed with a woman night after night, and I liked it. For the first time since living with Radha in Vancouver twenty years earlier, I had sex with a lady night after night, and liked it. For the first two months I did not hold back. The hounds were loose. To say we had a healthy sex life would be an understatement. It was so healthy it was almost kinda sick. I never really felt any loss of ojas even though I was constantly watching, constantly observing myself.

We never argued. The only time Jaya or her daughter Terry got upset with me at all was when their old cat Bella died. Because we lived in an upstairs flat there was a question of what to do with Bella's lifeless form. I suggested we bung the body into the proverbial gunny-sack, weigh it down with the proverbial brick and toss it in the proverbial nearby river. They really did not appreciate my glib idea, something about Bella not liking water, and we ended up burying the carcass in her favorite park on a dark, rainy night. Jaya did rather unfairly accuse me of jealousy when I complained about the parade of former boyfriends who marched through our place over those months. They fawned over her while barely acknowledging my presence.

After a couple of months, as Jaya began to hint at marriage, I began to hanker for India. Honestly I still felt no difference in my energy level. But I thought about it somewhat obsessively. I couldn't imagine going back to the ashram without holding my o for at least a month even if it was only psychological. So I stopped releasing ojas. I'm not certain that Jaya even noticed or cared. She certainly noticed the one-way airline ticket lying on the kitchen table one evening. But to her great credit she remained a true stoic British lady. It was perhaps for her just one more disappointment by one more guy in her life.

Pretty much as soon as I had returned, Mayama offered me a massage but I was so not interested. Otherwise, yes, I slipped back immediately into my same old routines, my same old business for the next long while until I got a call from my same old mom. "We're losing her! We're losing her!" That was all I could hear. I managed to call my brother a while later who explained what was happening more clearly. Apparently my sister had slipped into an irreversible coma following weeks of struggling with horrible migraines. I had to go.

Driving to Delhi during the monsoons in those days was not fun, not safe, but Devi and Rajesh insisted on accompanying me. There were regular land-slides. Rocks would come hurtling down the mountains at any time and we did come across a slide that blocked the road. That was near the Pundoh Pass, a stretch of gravel which was treacherous at the best of times. We walked over the boulders in the pouring rain and caught a taxi waiting on the other side. Unfortunately the driver had been on the move for three straight days and dog-tired. He wouldn't let me drive, insisted on continuing, wagging his head and saying: "If it is God's will..."

Somewhere between the time the guy narrowly missed a truck and very nearly sent us over a cliff I began to routinely swat him to keep him alert. He told Devi in Hindi that he was scared of me and well he should've been. We kept a close watch on him the whole way. We finally arrived in Delhi around four a.m., pulled up to our hotel and I grabbed the keys saying: "It's God's will that you sleep for a few hours."

By that time my sister had died. It must've been one helluva headache. As it happened I only had time for a shower before needing to get to the airport. I couldn't help but wonder what actually happened to her. It will remain a mystery. Was it her rather questionable upbringing that left her with emotional issues and migraines? Was it the meditation? Was it an undetected tumor or aneurism? I sort of go with the idea of it being a fine mixture of lousy childhood, a misunderstanding about meditation practice and probably a nasty tumor.

Whatever may have been the case I still had to fly. On the plane I was seated beside a cute little Indian girl. I felt terribly and unusually fortunate. I usually sat beside some humongous smelly person. I was ready to have a nice nap but almost predictably the cute little girl's family spirited her away and replaced her with a humongous smelly person, an uncle or maybe father.

One can easily imagine what the general atmosphere was like at my parents' apartment upon my arrival. My sister-in-law kept hollering: "It's not sposed to be like this, not sposed to be like this!" My mom was chain-smoking. Dad sat quietly, head down, and relations I hardly knew kept filing in and out. I was exhausted. Eventually I extricated myself from the general gnashing of teeth, lay down on a cot on the balcony and slept the sleep of the dead.

When I awoke I really didn't know where I was. And once I figured it out I wished I wasn't. The service was short although painful. The reception afterward was even more painful. An old lady who nobody seemed to know asked my mom why she smoked so much. Anybody who knew my mom at all began to tremble. Many tried to slither out of the room. Mom didn't answer but fumed, and the old lady foolishly persisted: "That can't be doing you any good." Now everyone was trying to leave. My brother and I looked at each other. We totally knew what was coming. "Have you ever tried to stop?," the stupid old lady asked. At that, dear old mom jumped out of her chair, threw her arms up and positively hollered: *"HAVE YOU EVER TRIED TO MIND YOUR OWN FUCKING BUSINESS!?"* The old lady fell backwards off her seat. Whoever was left in the room were holding their stomachs. My brother tried to calm mom down, a gallant gesture he immediately regretted.

The only nice part of that whole day and evening was the presence of an extremely hot lady who I made a point of sitting close to and chatting with. I had no idea who she was but I was transfixed, could hardly take my eyes off her, really wanted to get to know her, get close to her, make many babies with her. It came as a bit of a shock, therefore, to learn that she was a relative of mine. In fact it turned out she was my first cousin's very young teenage daughter. I'd been lusting after my cousin's teenage daughter.

The next day mom and dad had one of their mammoth arguments, both yelling and spluttering with eyes bulging, until my dad stormed out. I had just been about to go for a walk, had my jacket on, so we ended up walking down the street together and, for the first time I could ever recall, we kind of had a heart-to-heart talk during which I asked him if he had ever thought of divorce. He insisted in no uncertain terms that he never had and never would ever think of divorce. "Never never never." There was a silence during which I kept thinking he was a total jerk until he turned to me, actually smiled and said: "Of course you know I've thought of murder once or twice."

On 'Vipassanaforum.net', a fellow with the exotic name of Dick asks: "Occasionally when I sit I seem to develop a very heavy feeling in my head, particularly the back of my neck and in my temples. It's a kind of tight, tense feeling that ends up staying with me for some hours or even the whole day. After the meditation, it feels exactly like the onset of a nasty headache." In response to Nick, a fellow by the name of Jhana says: "The purpose of meditation is 'letting go.' In other words, meditation is a relaxation exercise. I discovered that I was building up tension in the background during meditation, that staying too long in a posture and forcing my concentration was counter-productive." Whatever may have been the case with my dear dead sister one thing was pretty sure: she was headed to a better place, and so was I. I was headed back to India.

Chapter 17

Relax Your Balls

A high-court judge visited the ashram from Delhi and of course Shyam had the whole satsang video-taped. The hall was filled as we all crowded in. Shyam talked a lot as usual; he introduced certain ones of us with tremendous credentials, asked a few people to speak. It was all pretty boring as far as I was concerned. Shyam asked the judge a few questions, one being: "What do you do, after hearing a case, if you can't make up your mind?" The judge launched into an excruciatingly long and detailed description of the process he goes through in order to make a judgment. After a while it was just too damn boring, tedious, even painful and mercifully Shyam interrupted.

"Hansraj!" he called out into the room. I jumped to my feet. I was sitting near the back of the crowded hall on the floor. I was wearing white kurta-pajama with my long, dark hair hanging down my back with rudraksh mala beads around my neck. Turning to the judge Shyam began: "This is Hansraj. He looks like a simple Kullu mountain man but his father is the main judge of Canada who has presided over many famous cases, such as when a nurse was accused of killing babies in a hospital." Then to me he said: "Hansraj what would your father do if he couldn't make up his mind about a case?" For some reason I knew exactly how to answer. "That's very easy sir. He would simply bring it up during dinner and his wife would tell him what to do." The crowd went wild and Shyam nearly fell off his seat laughing.

It was said, by whom I do not know, that there's an astrologically perfect full-moon time for a healing by Guru. At the appointed hour, with the moon illuminating the world, we all collected on the roof-top of the meditation hall while Shyam himself prepared some kheer, sweet rice, to be distributed during the ceremony. While it was cooking he told everyone to lie down on our backs in the Savasana pose to meditate. I was laying in between my friends Jaanki and Devi. Eventually Shyam began to speak. He began to lead us in a kind of guided meditation as part of the healing.

Shyam instructed us to put our attention on the toes, encouraged us to consciously relax them, then the feet as a whole. He instructed us to consciously relax our legs, our mid-section, our stomach and he slowly continued to lead us up through the body. Unfortunately when he got to the eyes, instead of saying: "Relax your eyeballs," he said: "Now relax your balls." As far as I know nobody reacted to that except for Jaanki and I who, for the life of us, could not stop giggling.

We just kept getting worse and worse. Shyam corrected himself but it was too late. Jaanki and I were completely out of control, rolling around, holding our stomachs, trying to be quiet. After a few moments I got up and ran off the roof. When Shyam went to check on the kheer he called me over from where I was sitting. He gave me two towels and told me to lift the huge bucket of the stuff off the fire and take it around the corner of the hall behind a tree out of sight. I had no idea why. Once there I put the bucket on some rocks while Shyam undid his dhoti and, smiling and winking at me, pissed into the kheer. Afterward he mixed it all and a few of us distributed a bit to each person on the roof while Shyam spoke of its powerful healing qualities.

Those were, by the way, the days when Shivambu Kalpa had become strangely popular in certain circles. The theory was simple enough: there were allegedly powerful healing properties in one's own urine and the practice of drinking the stuff could would should create tremendous health and vitality. The practice was made famous by Morarji Desai, Prime Minister of India from 1977 to 1979, who disingenuously declared that urine therapy was a perfect therapy for the millions of Indians unable to pay for medical care. He even wrote a gripping book called: 'The Miracles of Urine Therapy' and he did live to the ripe old age of ninety-nine. In his book Desai recommended that one ingest ones first pee of the day for best and most wondrous effects. I did actually try it, one time. I had a deuce of a time swigging it down and the only obvious effect it had was to make me feel a bit ill for the rest of that day.

The number of people at the ashram in those days had swelled to over two-hundred-and-fifty. The atmosphere had changed. It seemed rather unfocussed, getting a weee bit nuts. I had my hut up the hillside but I spent the nights down in Shyam's family compound. He mostly wasn't there. He stayed in his place, the old renovated cow-shed, which was beside the meditation hall. Although he was quite close to his three daughters Shyam didn't get along too well with his wife, Mataji. There's no doubt it was ridiculously difficult for a traditional Indian woman to share her husband with a gaggle of lovely western ladies. There's also no doubt she was a very difficult person. In many ways she reminded me of my own mother. Shyam and Mataji must've gotten along at some points in their marriage. They had the five children together after all. Shyam once told me he 'shot five arrows and hit the mark all five times.' I doubted that but it certainly wasn't my business.

I was supposedly acting as a night-watchman since there had been a bunch of robberies but really I was there to keep an eye on Shyam's eldest son. Makesh was out of control, not in his right mind. He smoked a lot of dope, sometimes railed against his dad, even insisted the CIA had abducted Shyam and replaced him with an imposter. The whole situation came to a head one night when Makesh and Shyam nearly had a fist-fight. I had to step in between the two and unfortunately a rubber water-hose that had been hanging down from the top of the roof got wrapped around Makesh's neck. It didn't look good. Mataji went mad, yelling and screaming at me, at Shyam, clutching her son and trying to get the hose off. He was choking and spluttering and turning all sorts of different colors until we could free the guy. The whole scene finally settled down and everyone went to their respective rooms. I sat in my little cupboard of a room in the dark but, at about two in the morning, Shyam walked in.

Once he walked in I lit a candle, only he quickly told me to blow it out. He just wanted to hide. Mataji was pacing the courtyard, still steaming, still fuming while Shyam and I talked in whispers. He was going on about how much better everything would've been if he had never married. I said: "But you often have said you realized the Self because of Mataji." To that he spat: "Oh I have to say something. My father made me marry. I tell you, if things get much crazier around here I'll just spread shit all over myself and then everyone will leave." Interestingly that's kinda what he ended up doing, metaphorically speaking.

In the book: 'Reflections on Talks with Sri Ramana Maharshi', Ramana is reported to have said: "Bramacharya is being in Brahman or living in Brahman. It has no connection with celibacy, as it is commonly understood. A real brahmachari finds bliss in Brahman, which is the Self. Why should he then look for other sources of happiness? In fact, emergence from the Self is the cause of all misery."

S.S.Cohen, the book's author, then reflects on that: "The inference, therefore, is that celibacy is granted to one who is ever in the 'brimful bliss of the Self'. Yet this inference must be wrong if it is taken as a general rule that the bramachari is always celibate. In fact, some of the most famous are known to have married and had children, some with possessions and some without. A further inference is that a real liberated bramachari is liberated also from rules and regulations, from all codes of ethical, religious and social conduct. Perhaps he is a law unto himself, and there is no knowing what he does or does not do." I find that so interesting and important, especially considering what was about to happen.

"Liberation," Ramana said, reported in the same book, "is a matter of fitness of mind. Married or unmarried, one can realize the Self, because the Self is here and now. Why think of yourself as a householder or a monk? The thought will haunt you. You will be only changing one thought for another. The mind is the obstacle, not the environment. Work performed with attachment is a shackle, whereas performed with detachment does not affect the doer. The latter is in solitude even while working. As for service, Realization of the Self is the greatest service that can be rendered to humanity. Therefore, the saints are helpful although they may dwell in forests. But, it should not be forgotten that solitude is not obtained in forests only, but even in towns, in the thick of worldly occupations. The help is imperceptible, but it is still there. A saint helps the whole of humanity unknown to it"

I'd known Sukhya forever, as she became a lovely young lady, as I became whatever I became, never actually imagined I'd end up in bed with her, ever. We'd always been close but didn't hang out together much. Well, she'd been asking me to visit but when I finally did drop over there were a couple of guys sitting in her room. So I just said 'hi' and 'bye' but she grabbed me on the road next day, insisted I go with her to the river. That seemed reasonable enough.

We hung out all afternoon swimming, chatting. We had a good time. Later we went back up to the ashram, realized Shyam was in the meditation hall so I went in, sat near the back. Sukhya came in and sat right beside me. That was mildly unsettling. Eventually I left but immediately discovered she was still right there with me. I told her I needed to head home to eat but she wanted to head up there with me and ok so I guess I could see where this was headed as we headed up the hill.

After dinner I announced that I was really tired, had to lie down and next thing I knew Sukhya was snuggled in so close you wouldn't have been able to get a piece of paper between us. At that point I demanded that she leave. Ok, no I didn't. Maybe I should've. Maybe I could've. Maybe I really wanted to. But nope. I wrapped my arms around, kissed each of her eyes and then softly kissed her lips. She asked me not to do that and I said: "Will you tell me what to do as well as what not to do?"

I have absolutely no idea why that was some sort of magical phrase that opened her right up. All I know is Sukhya seemed to melt. She began kissing me and I kissed her back. We kissed while feeling each other's bodies. Our clothes seemed to simply dissolve as we explored and experienced and before long were naked. Her nipples stiffened as my tongue circled, my cock was engorged and then I was on top of her. Around that time I asked myself: 'What the fuck are you doing? Are you a bramachari or simply a normal horny jerk?' The situation at that point did seem to clearly indicate I was the latter, as I continued kissing every inch of her tight young carcass happily, hungrily, even gratefully. I licked her stomach and easily spread her legs.

I began to lick and suck her cunt, circling her clit before working it softly. Sukhya was holding my head and moaning loudly. For a moment I came up and kissed her deeply, letting her taste her own juice before diving down to suck her clit again. After several minutes I could tell she was about to cum. Her breath quickened, her back began to arch. She was pulling my hair ruthlessly as I felt her beginning to spasm. And then I stopped. I just stopped. I don't exactly know why. It was maybe as though if I didn't give her an orgasm and I didn't actually fuck her then it was all ok, like it never happened. Whatever might've been my cockeyed reasoning I stopped.

I held onto Sukhya tightly as she settled down. I kissed her, told her how beautiful I thought she was. We lay there together for a while until eventually we got up, got dressed. It was well after dark by then so I walked her back down the hillside to her place. I passed her next day on the path. She was coming up from the river with some folks. I was headed down. She seemed a bit uptight, kind of scowled at me and I wondered if it was because of what I'd done or because of what I hadn't done.

I thought a lot about leaving in those last couple of years, a lot. Try as I might I could not re-kindle the sense of romance I had with the country, the mountains, sadhana, the ashram, even Shyam. I was just living my life and it seemed rather stagnant. Devi made dinner for me every evening, I played basketball every afternoon. My business was lucrative and easy. I had a big television, friends all around, a great dog. Life was really good. So I left.

Chapter 18

Saucy Lady

Once I was on the plane, I knew I wasn't going back. I stayed with Jaya's daughter for a few days in London and hardly an hour before I was to continue on to Toronto I got a call from a friend. Shakti had lived in Kullu for many years before falling in love with a British guy visiting the ashram. She left with him and had been living in London for about six months. "Leaving India after so long is not as easy as you may be thinking, Hansraj," Shakti said. "You really should think about it carefully before making up your mind." I thanked her for the call and the advice, but I also basically told her I knew what I was doing. She tried to repeat the warning, but I was not really listening.

That same day, I landed at my parents' apartment in Toronto. Dinner, such as it was, had just ended when I received the call. Yes, that call. It was from a Toronto lady, Sherry, I vaguely knew from her recent visit to India. I was surprised that she even had my parents' number. She asked if I was sitting down. I said I was, although I really wasn't. She said: "Shakti's dead." Then I sat down. Apparently Shakti collapsed in the shower but nobody ever really knew what happened or why. After the phone call and after my folks shuffled off down the hall to play 'Bridge' with some friends I spent the evening trying unsuccessfully not to think about Shakti and our last conversation. I read through my dad's forbidden private papers until I fell asleep.

After another surreal day with the folks, by the later afternoon I decided to go out for a walk. First I did walk, then hopped a bus and eventually took a subway right downtown. I strolled up and down Yonge Street, took in the sights and sounds of the city and, after dark, slipped into an old haunt of mine from a hundred years back: 'The Brass Rail'. It's a strip club, kind of sleazy, kind of depressing, kind of perfect for me at that precise time. It was different than I remembered, yet not so different.

I nursed a beer and watched some very beautiful girls dance very badly. Of course I remembered how amazing a dancer my old girlfriend Elizabeth, Zana, had been. The girls I watched that night, while undeniably lovely, were undeniably terrible dancers. Muscle-bound studs lingered here and there, bouncers or security guards of some sort. Lap-dancing was a new phenomenon to me. Each lady in turn offered me one or tried to coax me into a special, private room. I was completely uninterested.

One lady, however, seemed to be cool with just chatting, didn't even offer me a lap-dance. We just sat together a long while talking. I asked her about her life. She was engaging and even funny. Eventually she said she'd have to go or she'd get into trouble just hanging out with one customer. But she added that we could hang out for a while in one of the private rooms.

The private room was a cubicle up on the second floor and as soon as we got in the lady said she would have to dance a bit because the rooms were monitored. That was different from what I had been led to understand hardly a moment or two earlier but we continued a conversation of sorts even while she stripped off her skimpy costume and gyrated all over me. She even fondled my dick over my pants. I was not even the slightest little bit hard. My cock was as limp as a rope lying on the ground although she continued to dance, gyrate and massage my crotch.

After about three songs I suggested we cut the crap. I wanted to leave. She was perfectly ok with that, slipped back into her halter-top and g-string and as we walked down the stairs one of the Neanderthal security guys presented me with a bill of three-hundred-and-seventy-five dollars. It was really just a scrap of paper with the number written on it. I complained that I had no idea I was being charged for her time, that I had not been told anything about it in advance, quite the opposite actually, and I refused to pay. The engaging, friendly little lady meanwhile had undergone an incredible transformation somewhere between the room and the stairs. She became a monster with eyes made of fire who growled that I had better pay if I valued my health. It was of course an expensive lesson.

I didn't just go to Ottawa a few days later. I ran to Ottawa. Or, more precisely, I ran away from Toronto, from my family. There was a family wedding that I was expected to return in time for. However, in the back of my mind was an idea to ask for a job at an Ottawa jewelry store I briefly worked in nineteen years earlier. I only knew one person in the Ottawa area by then. Lauri had visited India a few years back and had recently sent me a message that I'd be welcome to visit with her and her house-mate. She was good enough to pick me up at the train station and drove me to their place. I had no idea she lived way outside of the city, in Wakefield, Quebec, but I instantly fell in love with the village. I stayed with Lauri for a few days, then house-sat for friends of hers. All I had to do was take care of their house and their dog.

It felt spectacular being in the village, totally loved the people, the river, the house, the dog but on about the third day of house-sitting and dog-walking I threw my back out, way out. I could barely move. The dog got her exercise after that by chasing a stick I'd throw from my prone position on the grass. At one point I went to sit in a lawn chair, its cloth ripped as I fell into it and I was stuck, unable to extricate myself for hours. It put a whole new meaning to the old adage: 'your ass in a sling.' Lauri brought food and medicine. I slithered around the yard and house until I decided I'd better phone my folks.

As soon as I heard mom's gravelly voice however my sphincter tightened right up, my stomach lurched; my eyes flew open as though I'd seen a ghost. When I told her that I hurt my back she growled: "Well you'd better do something quick buster because you have your cousin's wedding to attend and you need to look for a job." I could always count on mom. Needless to say that's when I decided to make Wakefield home. The jewelry thing didn't work out right away but I found a job pumping gas at a local station. In India I was a well-respected wealthy business-man and supposedly a spiritually advanced bramachari yogi. In Wakefield I was a lowly gas jockey and I was perfectly ok with that. The new modern western world meanwhile presented me with a pretty stiff learning curve.

During the more than two decades I spent in India the banking system progressed from trading cows and hiding currency under false floorboards to actual banks. During my last several years there in fact I placed what money I had in the Bank of Patiala.

One had to enter the bank by stepping over a chain left for some unknown reason always across the front doorway. A very small man with a very large rifle sat just inside. The rifle was an ancient, double-barreled affair slung proudly over his shoulder. A sign hanging above the counter read: 'Please Count Yor Monys Befor Leving.' There were no computers of course and simple withdrawals or deposits could take the better part of a morning.

The day I was leaving for Canada I asked to withdraw most of my funds which amounted to some fifty-thousand rupees, just under two thousand dollars Canadian. That may not sound like a king's ransom but a normal withdrawal would consist of no zeros at all made by a simple hill-person in town purchasing sugar for a special occasion or getting a tooth pulled following a special occasion.

After some discussion amongst themselves the teller came back to the counter. "That will not be possible sir. Very sorry," he said wagging his head from side to side smiling. Returning two days later was out of the question and so after some further negotiations we agreed I could indeed have my money, in bundles of fives and tens. The fellow with the rifle was sent to the market for bags.

In Canada I discovered banking had progressed without waiting for me. In my quest for respectability I acquired all the right cards and made all the right moves. However, when I went to the office in Hull to pick up a license-plate for my new really old car, I faced a huge dilemma. In order to finally grab the plate, sitting on the counter like the Holy Grail itself, I had to pay two-hundred-and-seventy-five bucks, cash. I had handed the severe-looking lady my Visa card as I swelled with pride but she wouldn't take it. I offered her a debit card. She refused. I didn't have a check or enough cash so she, with a show of tremendous forbearance, looking like wanting nothing more than to kick the family dog, suggested I go use the cash machine in the next building and come back. I had never used a cash machine. I knew I would eventually. I just wanted to wait for the right moment and that wasn't it. With a lot of people waiting at the license office and several waiting behind me at the cash machine that was most certainly not the right time.

There seemed to be a few slots and I kept trying to stick the card in each of them. The lighting was poor and I was under pressure. I tried pushing the card into one or another aperture until I finally realized two of the slots were just lines. Of course I looked mentally challenged as I tried to force my card into any mark that might've been the right one. I turned the card up and down and around, no doubt looking even more 'special' until the beast finally grabbed the thing.

With the card mercifully deposited in its proper receptacle I next had to read the simple instructions. People came and went from the next machine while behind me the folks either giggled or groaned as they crowded in. My machine asked if I wanted FRENCH or english. The arrow seemed to point between the buttons. I thought I pressed for english but got FRENCH, had to start again. More giggles. More groans. I knew my secret pin code but made a couple more mistakes before figuring the whole thing out. I punched in my desired amount, waited, waited, got my card back, waited and then got rejected. Nobody likes rejection. I tried everything again and I was rejected again. A voice from the now raucous crowd behind called out in a sarcastic tone, "It's gotta be in multitudes of twenty." I thanked the man without turning around, consoled by the thought that I'd probably never see any of them again, finally got the money and beetled away.

As I re-entered the license office, people were looking down-right nasty. The lady behind the counter had her head in her hands. I paid my money, grabbed the plates and drove off into the new world.

The internet, another great challenge, had snaked its way up to Kullu hardly a month after my departure. Had it arrived a month earlier, I might not have ever left. Be that as it may, once I was settled in the new world I got a refurbished computer, scored some internet access and proceeded to check out every site from local news to porn. It opened me up to new ideas, experiences and a heck of a lot of weird shit.

Isolated in my little West Quebec cabin, working long hours pumping gas at the station and hardly knowing a soul, I became particularly fond of internet chat rooms. It was kind of nice to talk with other obviously disenfranchised, faceless humans. One night I was in a relatively liberal sort of chat room called 'Hot Coffee – Warm Hearts' when someone 'whispered' to me. That's a mechanism whereby one might carry on a private conversation within the chat room. She, he or it wrote: "Hey Tercel, (my chosen user name,) if you wanna DO me, click on my name, click hard!"

Having recently spent twenty-five years in a place that discouraged ladies from showing bare shoulders or ankles, and not having had much of a chance to 'do' any of them, I clicked. In fact, I clicked quite hard even though I couldn't even find her name on the room's members' list. I actually kept clicking but it was no good. She never responded. I was obviously not going to be able to do her. I had been duped. As well, my email inbox soon filled with messages ranging from 'teen sluts' to 'naked celebrities,' 'horny couples' to 'hidden cameras.'

While I certainly learned that new lesson I still wandered through all different chat rooms. On one occasion in a free-spirited chat room called 'Bi-sexual Coffee Shop' a conversation between a guy called Fishfry and a girl called SaucyLady caught my attention. Saucylady kept saying she could never fall in love again because she's been 'demolished.' I felt Fishfry was not being very understanding, sensitive or supportive. So when Saucylady said she'd still have sex, but never love, my eyebrows went up and I felt compelled to jump in. It sounded like good sound logic to me and decided I could be of much more help to her than Mr. Fishfry. It's not that I was really hoping for sex with no strings attached, but...

"What kind of name is Fishfry anyway?" I whispered to him.

"Each to his own," was his deft reply.

"Did you have fish for dinner?" I badgered. "Do you like fishing? Do you live by a lake or an ocean? Do you have webbed feet?"

Then I saw "Bye, Saucylady. I'm tired and some guy named Tercel is badgering me."

Then, as always happened when someone logged off, a line in the chat box stated: 'Fishfry has left the conversation.'

Saucylady wrote: "Tercel, were you badgering Fishfry?"

"No. Not at all. He must've just had bigger fish to fry."

"Ha ha, LOL you're funny," she typed.

So I plunged right in.

"What happened, Saucy One, that demolished you?"

What ensued was a two-hour conversation that held within it some of the most powerful moments I had shared with a lady in my adult life which of course says a lot about my adult life. Suffice it to say we laughed, she cried, there became a promise of something bordering on real depth until it came time to describe ourselves. She sounded fine to me. But then, I'm not sure if it was the 48-year-old part, the 25 years in India thing or the gas station attendant situation but all of a sudden I saw: 'Saucylady has left the conversation.' I was stunned. I was, in fact, demolished. I stared at the screen for ages until I swore I'd never fall in love again.

I did return to that same chat room the very next night, looked on the list of names there. No sign of Saucylady. I typed in, "Has anyone seen Saucylady?" A few minutes later I typed it in again. To my surprise I got a response from a lady who called herself Playtex.

"I hope you find your lady, Tercel," she wrote.

"Thanks," I responded. "Why did you choose that name?"

"I just liked it," she wrote.

"It's a stretch but works for me," I replied.

"Ha ha, you're funny."

What ensued was an hour-long conversation that held within it some of the most powerful moments I had shared with a lady, well, since the previous night, until she whispered to me.

"Tercel, can I ask you a question?" which meant two, because that was already one question.

"Sure."

"What should I do, Tercel, if I've fallen in love with someone on the internet?"

I thought before answering, keeping in mind the rather unlikely possibility that she might be referring to me.

"I guess you should ask him what he's feeling. What've you got to lose?"

Then, without warning I saw: 'Playtex has left the conversation.' And I was demolished, again.

As the years passed, sleeping in my parents' apartment on my visits from Wakefield became a tremendous challenge. Mom slept in the large master bedroom on one side while my dad was delegated to the den on the other. It wasn't because he snored. It was because she snored. I never heard anything quite like it before or since. You really couldn't get away from it anywhere in the apartment and I had to sleep on the sofa in the living room between the two rooms. You might say i was stuck between a rock and a hard place. Suffice it to say the general atmosphere was oppressive.

I vividly recall one winter visit specifically for a few good reasons. Firstly, I had pulled a chest muscle trying to do too many push-ups earlier in the day on their cold balcony. So I was even more uncomfortable than usual that night. Secondly, while I tried to get some sleep my mom woke up and wandered out into the living room looking for her cigarettes, buck naked. It's an image that still haunts me from time to time. But I also remember the occasion because of what happened later.

I tried to sleep but eventually I just sat up and began to meditate. My head was throbbing and my chest hurt. I kept envisioning my old mom naked. I kept wishing I was home. Nevertheless a great meditator observes whatever's happening without trying to cling onto the pleasant or get away from the unpleasant. A great meditator practices equanimity, being the watcher, the uninvolved observer. After a few minutes of that however I thought "fuck this shit", got dressed and went for a walk.

I walked for quite a while along icy sidewalks until I found myself in front of the 'North Toronto General Hospital'. Seeing the lights and activity and thinking it might be nice to sit down somewhere warm for a few minutes I decided to go in. I was immediately escorted to a counter where a tired-looking woman asked me a few questions. When I produced my Quebec health card she frowned. However, when she asked what the problem was, for lack of anything else to report I said I was having chest pains and that changed everything. I had no idea what effect it would have. Her head bolted up, she called to someone in the next room and within moments, with a large room full of folks in various states of discomfort patiently waiting, I was whisked through to an inner area, slapped onto a gurney, electrodes attached to my chest and a needle stuck in my arm. I had just wanted to sit down somewhere warm.

A nurse came in and told me that I would need to stay there for at least a couple of hours. I could hardly explain that I was simply walking the streets because I couldn't get the image of my naked mother out of my head. So I settled back and decided to make the best of it. Soon I drifted off into what would become a wonderful sleep/meditation. A nurse would come once in a while and we would smile at each other. I heard somebody crying nearby at one point and I felt tremendous empathy but it wasn't a terrible feeling. In fact I felt kind of at home, comfortable.

As the morning approached a doctor came in, announced that I was fine. He suspected it was just a pulled muscle in my chest. I could go. I was almost sorry to leave. However, walking into daylight I appreciated the feeling of the cold air on my face, glad to have good health. And when I arrived in front of my parents' apartment door I took a deep breath, prayed there'd be enough oxygen to go around and then I entered. A little later on, sitting around the breakfast table, mom asked how my night had been and I told her it had been really very nice. That seemed to make her happy.

Chapter 19

What Happens in India
Stays in India.

In retrospect, sitting in my home in Wakefield I guess I felt
life as I knew it had been slowly unraveling at the ashram for
quite some time. The village and large parts of the valley were
no longer beautiful or charming. The population growth along
with unbridled construction took care of that. The ashram itself
was over-flowing with all manner of devotees, pseudo devotees,
wild, wondrous and weird devotees. The place got kinda crazy
and perhaps Shyam was in effect spreading dung all over himself, metaphorically speaking, just as he said he would. Those
were very likely a couple of reasons for my leaving, at least semi-
consciously. I don't honestly know for sure.

There were loosely a couple of groups who initially turned
against Shyam: a few smokers, dopers who just wouldn't stop
even though he threatened to have them tossed, and there were a
few quite vocal folks who genuinely felt mistreated emotionally,
sexually or both. Once it began, however, there was a snow-ball
effect. Some accusations were almost certainly true; others I
know were false, and ridiculous. There were haters coming outta
the wood-work, some who took it on as a personal crusade, to

expose him for the devil he was. Many more would not entertain the slightest possibility of Shyam, guru, being considered less than a God. And then there was me.

To me Shyam was a devil and a God. He was both. The truth in my opinion does not lie somewhere in-between the extremes. He was both. He was all of it. He could not be trusted to behave according to 'normal' moral sensibilities. He certainly could not be trusted to behave according to anyone's conditions or expectations. He could be trusted to show you over time what real freedom is. You just might not like it, at least not all of it. I recall sitting with him at some point during the '70s as a letter was read out from a guy who had done something terrible. I don't even recall what it was but I clearly recall Shyam laughing, clapping and exclaiming: "Oh he's sooo free!" And I also clearly recall being shocked. "That's freedom?" I asked incredulously. "Sure," he responded. "You couldn't do it. He's freer than you."

I left nearly two years before the 'fit hit the shan', before the accusations, before the nasty website and the newspaper articles. The fellow who wrote the articles, John Stackhouse, whom I nicknamed 'Steakhouse', called me up one day in Wakefield to get a statement for the story he was about to publish. I told him I had nothing to add because I wouldn't say anything negative. Steakhouse said he just wanted the truth. "No you don't," I responded. "You want to write a typically sensational article about yet another Indian guru sexually abusing his innocent followers. You've been fed a whole bunch of negative shit and you have a very definite agenda."

Steakhouse asked whether it was true or not that Shyam had sexual relations with his students. I pointed out that I don't peek into peoples' windows so I won't venture an opinion on that. He insisted he wanted a statement from me specifically because he knew I lived over twenty-five years rather closely with the man. "Ok listen John," I offered. "If you really wanna write a half-decent article at least print my statement: 'Swami Shyam has been the most life-supportive person in my life and I will always be grateful to him.'" Needless to say my statement did not show up in his scathing article splashed across the front pages of the 'Globe and Mail'.

The truth of the matter, in my semi-humble and somewhat less than fully informed opinion, lies buried somewhere in amongst all the ugly claims of Shyam's accusers and the beautiful opinions of those who would've followed him to the ends of the earth. I always knew how free he was. It's what attracted me in the first place. It's what attracted all of us. He was a hurricane, an earthquake, a wild-man. He was a sunny day, a breath of fresh air and a savior. It really depends on who you talk to and when. My dilemma is that the few who hate Shyam will hate me for speaking well of him, while all those who love him will hate me for speaking ill of him.

I'll try to further explain only why it's a complicated issue. It should in no way be viewed as an attempt to condone or brush aside allegations of sexual misconduct by Shyam. That's not where I'm at at all. I've heard the term 'spiritual narcissist' lately and I kinda like that. Adding a word to the label of narcissist is fitting because it suggests an extra level of complication.

Firstly, nobody was compelled to stay, at all. Secondly, he never hit any person or animal ever. Was he verbally abusive at times? Oh yeah absolutely. Was he a hypocrite at times? Oh yeah absolutely. Would he even lie at times? Oh yeah absolutely. And the result was that so many gained a thick skin, a crazy sense of humor, even an expanded understanding of life. So many people around him became strong and free. Those who couldn't or wouldn't handle it, well, they'll have quite a different opinion and I can't say they're wrong, not at all. Theirs would be a perfectly valid point-of-view.

So what about the sex? Well, yeah, what about the sex? Did he attract or coax female devotees into some manner of sexual relations over the years? Almost certainly he did. Did his female devotees attract or coax him into having some manner of sexual relations over the years? Almost certainly they did. Of course I'm aware that girls and ladies are bombarded by the desires of boys and men. They're chatted-up, cajoled, coaxed and often creeped-upon by guys who all too often cross a blurry line into out-right abuse. I get it. And whatever might've been the case in this case Shyam was the man, the guru. He was in a position of authority. So by any 'normal' western standard of moral responsibility and culpability he would almost certainly be considered guilty as charged. Cuff him. Take him away. I will not stand in your way. Oops, too late.

Before condemning him outright and completely, however, along with all his devotees, it'd be useful to try to understand something I touched upon earlier: Shyam was one of those rare beings with an ability to open up hearts and minds to states of consciousness not ever normally experienced, and not just intellectually but viscerally, directly. In Sanskrit it's called 'shaktipath.' That's partly why it's a complicated issue. In those early days we considered any contact with Guru, with Shyam, in any manner, an aid to enlightenment, a blessing. As well one has to consider the rather huge number of intelligent, highly aware, loving men and women who to this day continue to adore the memory of the man. Are they all in fact brain-washed idiots? Or is there more than one way to look at the issue?

As far as I know, every guy in Kullu was kept in the dark in regard to the extent of Shyam's clandestine activities. Personally, I may have vaguely suspected but none of the ladies ever breathed a word to me until much later. All those ladies, even the one I was intimately involved with and deeply in love with, was perfectly happy to keep us guys perfectly happy in our ignorance. He's even since been accused of having inappropriate sexual contact with one under-age girl. I don't know of course and I won't venture any more of a guess than I've already made. He may have been a spiritual narcissist, or maybe just a horny Indian guy, but he was also guru. In hind-sight, I do wonder if I would've done anything differently. I honestly don't know, perhaps not. But I'm not overjoyed about the mess he left behind. Or perhaps it's perfect considering how much he loved shaking the very foundations of our ideas. The fact remains that I had a deep affection and respect for the man. And I still can't help feeling incredibly grateful for some great years and the role he played in my life.

'Women Accuse Agama Yoga Founder Swami Vivekananda Saraswati of Sexual Assault.' www.medium.com. July 24, 2018.

Dear Nathan; In regard to our discussion, I feel my psychologist put her finger on the Swami problem precisely. In spite of me pointing out that there were two sides, that ladies were positively lining up to be with Swamiji, she said that what happened is an abuse of power and authority, full stop. It is not two sided when in such a position of authority. One's ability to throw off pheromones or more, no matter how many women throw themselves at ones feet, it is the duty and responsibility of such a one to say no. That is why teachers and doctors are forbidden to cross that line. It made complete sense to me finally. I would like to know what you think. Sincerely; Mathew.

Dear Mathew; Thank you for sharing this and I'm glad you're clear about the issue. Your psychologist did not however bring any major clarity to me. I don't disagree with her but the issue as far as I'm concerned remains somewhat murky, as clear as mud. If one were to confine ones remarks to teachers, doctors or virtually anyone in positions of power and authority... other than highly developed siddha mahatmas, rishis, yogis, masters, saat gurus, I would agree whole-heartedly. I do agree. My only question has to do with the strange and enigmatic aforementioned group. With all due respect, those beings, few though they may be, almost certainly cannot be understood by your psychologist. All I continue to say is that the issue is complicated. Having said all that, I really must add that I personally lean way more toward the opinion of your psychologist than to any other rationale.

Be that as it may, there just seem so many more stories these days concerning sexual abuse by bathdurds in positions of power than ever before. Whether it's within the clergy or by teachers, doctors, husbands, fathers, entertainers, judges, presidents or great gurus, all sorts of stories are coming out. Obviously, it's actually a tremendously old story. The simple fact is that phenomenon, like poverty, like wars, like all manner of unkindness-es, will probably never really stop until the peoples of the world, all people understand, really understand, that we're essentially one life, that to hurt anyone else is to hurt one's own self.

Chapter 20

Back To The Future

Meanwhile, my head-space shifted exactly on my fiftieth birthday. Hardly a few minutes after waking that morning I realized I was not only finished looking for a relationship, I really no longer cared. I was back. I was satisfied with my situation just the way it was. In fact I preferred it.

That was a sunny Sunday morning. I sat outside reading the newspaper, drinking a coffee, appreciating how lucky it was that my mission had failed. Freedom felt like a drug. When the phone rang I almost floated in to answer. The sound of the caller's voice, however, threw me back to earth with a thud. 'Fuck,' I said to myself. I had clean forgotten about the date I made for that day. It was a lady who'd contacted me earlier in the week, attracted to my profile simply because I seemed to be a spiritual man. Apparently she was a very spiritual lady. She had no photo on her profile and her concepts raised more red flags for me than I could count.

For example, she told me she had no hair. I asked if she meant short hair or actually no hair. Her response definitely made an impression on me. She told me she had more hair on her legs than on her head. She never wore jewelry. She never used makeup. I'm really not sexist but good or bad I am a pretty normal guy. Still I agreed to meet in Wakefield, something I normally avoided when getting together with a lady from the internet. Unfortunately she loved the village and insisted on coming up from Gatineau. It was all against my better judgment. I agreed to meet on Sunday in Wakefield, where everyone knew me, with a lady who had more hair on her legs than her head.

If I had 'call display' I never would've picked up the phone that morning. She asked what I was doing and I innocently told her I was reading the newspaper. She proudly stated that she never reads the newspaper, listens to the radio or watches TV. Aside from the small fact that she had just put me down for the apparently unspiritual habit of keeping abreast of the world and community events, it was yet another red flag, another large, bright red fluttering flag. I did not want to meet her anywhere I might be known so I suggested Sandy's Pizza Hut but my date vetoed the suggestion due to the fact that smoking was allowed there. So I offered to meet at Chez Eric. I was a regular there in those days because it was vegetarian but I just couldn't think of any other place. I've never been good under pressure. However, again, she nixed the idea. That surprised me. I pointed out that smoking was not allowed there. She countered by saying that smoking was allowed on the terrace and in the yard.

"So let me understand" I said. "You will not go where smoking is allowed even outside?"

"I don't allow smoking around me at all, ever!"

Then I had a rather infrequent moment of intelligence. I said: "But I smoke." Of course I didn't smoke, hadn't smoked in about thirty years.

"You smoke!?" she exclaimed.

"Like a chimney."

She pointed out that my profile had 'non-smoker' written on it but I quickly retorted that I started a few months back and couldn't stop.

"Then we can't meet," she announced.

"It's my loss," I said finally.

She was not pleased, suggested I phone her when I kicked the dirty habit and I said she'd be the first to know. And that turned out to be one of the best birthdays of all time.

Lucia came along soon after that but she was just a mistake that lasted a few months. We did meet on the internet even though I stopped looking for dates. I just used to sift through profiles out of boredom really or habit. I had no life. Once in a while I'd post a comment on someone's page, usually something glib or funny and that's how we met. I made a silly comment and she responded immediately. We began chatting and at some point during the conversation Lucia mentioned how disappointed she was that a friend had deserted her for the evening. For some reason I volunteered to fill in.

We met in the Byward Market for coffee and had a good time. Lucia was a petite, pretty lady from Peru, much younger than I. She was smart, articulate with straight, light-colored hair, dark eyes, an easy way about her. We ended up just hanging out all evening at the coffee shop, strolling through the market before I walked her to the parking garage. We kissed and it was hot. Lucia was pressed up against the car door as we kissed more passionately, as I explored her body a bit with my hands. She was wearing a rather light dress tied in the back and it was actually coming off. She may have wanted me to go for it right then and there. I don't know. But strangely I didn't really feel up to the task anyway.

I drove down to Lucia's place in Gatineau the next night and the night after that, and the night after that. We totally wanted to have the full experience only every time I stopped to put a condom on I'd lose my erection. I didn't know it then but that was one of the first symptoms of a not so 'Benign Prostatic Hyperplasia' or enlarged prostate. Had anybody checked the garbage they woulda noticed all the condoms and concluded we were screwing like a couple of rabbits. The reality was, after a week of trying I hadn't entered her once. Obviously not being able to fuck her was a tremendous concern. I called my friend Ray in Los Angeles.

Ray told me I needed something called 'Viagra'. I had never heard of that. It was a revelation to me and I begged him to send me a few pills. He finally agreed to send me one pill to try, one little pill which arrived next day in a ridiculously large Fed Ex box at my place of work. My employer handed it to me while I was selling an engagement ring to a young couple. He totally wanted to know what was in the box but I just threw it quickly under my desk and carried on. I went to visit Lucia that evening. I took half the pill on my way to her place in Aylmer, as per Ray's instructions. I was excited. Unfortunately, almost classically, she had a headache. I kept repeating to myself: 'You couldn't even make stuff like this up' during that rather uncomfortable night.

Anyway, I took the other half of the pill as I drove over next evening and we did it right in the hallway. We didn't even get into bed or onto a sofa. We didn't fall onto the carpet. I was hard as soon as we started kissing so I just turned her around in the hallway, lifted her dress, took her panties down, slipped on a condom and fucked her against the wall.

Yeah, we had a great sex life for sure after that. But I never told Lucia I took Viagra before each and every time I'd come over. I didn't need much. A quarter of a pill would do it. A half would be a helluva night. Viagra turned me into a young stud-muffin, gave me full control. I could screw all night and never lose a drop of semen/ojas. Ray told me I should never ever ever ever tell the lady I was taking Viagra ever ever because if I did, as he put it, I would never ever own my erection again.

Our relationship, while no doubt based somewhat on a lie, blossomed. I loved her cute little daughter; we all got together a few times a week. I'd stay over at her place often and there was even some talk of marriage. I couldn't quite warm up to the marriage idea for a couple of obvious reasons. Firstly, Lucia had told me from the start that I wasn't what she was looking for. Secondly, I would've had to admit I wasn't quite the stud she thought I was. I liked how she'd say: "I've never been fucked like this in my life." I didn't want to burst that bubble.

Then one night I decided to drive over just to give her a rose. Lucia had insisted I not come that night because she was tired and needed to sleep. So I thought it'd be terribly romantic to drive down to Gatineau, give her the rose, a kiss, then get back in my truck and drive home. As I approached her place, however, I saw a rather large black BMW in the driveway, so I just turned around and began driving home. After about a block I stopped to think it over. I turned to just drive around the block once, take another look but when I got to the house I couldn't help myself. I parked, went to the door and rang the bell.

Lucia was dressed in an incredible slinky low-cut evening gown. I could see a guy sitting at the dining-room table. There were candles lit. It wasn't too hard to figure out what was going on. Her little dog was excited to see me, jumped into my arms. Lucia wasn't quite as excited and didn't jump into my arms. I smiled: "I guess you'd like me to leave." She was completely freaked out and just nodded. Instead of leaving however I handed her the rose and walked into the dining room, sat down and began to chat with the guy.

Lucia's daughter was staying with her dad that night so I guess Lucia had a whole sleep-over planned for her and the new guy who, btw, had no idea who I was. I just said I was an old family friend. While Lucia quietly freaked he and I actually had an ok time. That guy was exactly what she had originally been looking for: worked for the government, drove a big BMW, smoked, drank, ate meat, French, young. He was perfect.

Eventually I excused myself and Lucia walked me to the door. I gave her a hug, told her not to worry, just have fun. Strangely, the only part that ever really bothered me was not seeing her daughter much anymore. Also I secretly decided after that I'd never lie about myself again.

Although her new boyfriend looked good on paper, apparently he didn't look so good in real life, at least after a while. That's the funny thing about holding on too tightly to concepts. Anyway Lucia was soon single again, kind of depressed and, while not inclined to slip back in to any sort of romantic relationship, I remained a friend. One day I got a weird idea that a sex-toy and a video would make a funny and timely gift.

I heard of a place in centre-town called 'Venus Envy' where, after entering, I was shocked to see shelf upon shelf of plastic or hard rubber cocks of all different shapes and sizes. It was frankly a little over-whelming. A young pretty girl approached. I asked her to make a suggestion and she said: "Well, you don't wanna get one bigger than you are 'cause you don't want your girlfriend to get used to that. Then she won't be satisfied with you." So I grabbed a humongous nine or ten-inch dildo and said: "Ok then this one will be fine." The girl laughed as I put it back and snatched a tiny one, maybe two inches long. "Ok, ok, then this one." It made her laugh even more.

In the end I chose an appropriately-sized rather modest one, not that it mattered, along with a video and the sales-girl wrapped it all up. It turned out to be a great fun retail experience. My wonderful gift was well received but somehow seemed to represent a kind of exclamation-mark on our relationship and I've hardly seen her since.

My next and almost certainly my final attempt at nuptial bliss was Sharman, the kindest, nicest lady you'd ever have the pleasure to know. She supposedly knew who and what I was but inexplicably stuck around anyway. In fact she even married me, for whatever reason, although not for long. I loved Sharman but I was not in love with her. That ship had sailed long ago. And while loving someone may be a purer form of love than being in love, it doesn't necessarily make for the great stereotypical marriage, at least not in our case. Within a year Sharman realized she'd made a horrible horrible mistake.

We met at a flakey new-age place in Ottawa called 'The Maclaren Centre.' It was a place where you could have reiki or massage, listen to crystal singing bowls or learn to talk to the angels. One of the owners of the place, a self-proclaimed angel communicator, would actually greet her clients wearing wings clipped onto her shoulders. The place was nuts and I liked it a lot. Sharman was volunteering there. I had set up some show-cases filled with spiritual art, statues and stuff, a business I was just beginning. In lieu of rent I taught meditation each week with any money going to the centre. Even once I opened my shop in Wakefield and stopped frequenting the centre, Sharman and I continued to get together. I liked her. She was young and cute, incredibly good-natured. She was a vegetarian and a meditator. What could possibly go wrong?

Sitting in my shop one day I emailed, as I often did, to tell her I was coming in to town next day and suggested getting together for coffee. Sharman agreed but added she wanted to make it quite clear that she did not want a relationship. After reading that, I was taken aback, literally, sat in my chair and thought about how to respond. Eventually I wrote: "Who asked you? If we do get together for coffee tomorrow I suggest you stick to decaf." After a while she simply wrote: "LOL." That was the way it was with us for over a year, until Sharman actually admitted one day to my utter surprise that in fact she did want a relationship with me, apparently had for a long time. Even then it took a while because I honestly didn't know what to do.

Anyway, we did manage to consummate our love, with some patience and modern medical assistance, ended up married, living in Wakefield, even got a dog. Almost as soon as we got him our dog Gaia got smudged by a truck and, because it was a Sunday afternoon, I had to drive to Ottawa, to the twenty-four-hour emergency veterinarian clinic. Sharman was beside herself with worry. I promised to phone as soon as I knew how he was. Anyway, the dog wasn't actually in too bad shape. I called and reported that Gaia was ok but that the doctor wanted to keep me overnight for observation. Sharman being Sharman, asked how the dog was gonna get home. She's a simple, kind-hearted woman but unfortunately or perhaps fortunately I'm not so simple or so kind-hearted and, while we remain great friends, we were truly a ridiculous married couple.

So one day Sharman trundled out the back door of the big house we owned, over to the tiny little six-by-ten cabin I actually spent ninety percent of my days AND nights, poked her head in the door and announced that she was leaving. I asked if I could come along. She laughed of course but said: "No, I'm leaving YOU." I knew that, of course, and leave she did. Eventually we even got divorced, following a great visit to India together, and the lawyer said it was the strangest divorce he'd ever presided over. When I asked why he remarked: "Well, you're here to sign the papers but you're holding hands."

Chapter 21

Missing Me

At mom's ripe old age of eighty-six, after a lifetime of chain-smoking, dad decided it was actually bad for her health. He cut her off. Since she was house-bound by that time and being pretty darn sure she'd die quickly without her ciggies, I became a kind of drug dealer. Really I wasn't totally concerned about her probable early demise but it just felt so wrong. As well, Alzheimer had changed her. It would be over-stating the fact to say she had become sweet and lovable. It would however be certainly correct to say she had become tolerable and bearable. Frankly I was kind of enjoying the change.

Every few weeks mom would call me in Wakefield and the sound of that gravelly voice would make the hairs on the back of my neck stand straight up. That voice could wake the dead. She would growl: "Nathan I'm missing you." Loosely translated it meant that she was running out of cigarettes. I would have to drive all the way to Toronto to slip her a carton or two which she'd puff away on secretly when dad was out or in her bathroom. Our relationship flourished and we grew so much closer than ever before.

Unfortunately, while I was on a six-week visit to India, poor mom couldn't get her ciggies and, sure enough, ended up in hospital. It didn't look good for the old girl. I hurried back from India a few days early, she rallied and so I returned home to Wakefield. However, late the very next afternoon I got a call from a nurse at the hospital who said that I had better get there immediately if I wanted to see my mother alive again. So I had dinner, watched a basketball game on television and went to bed.

Although mom was expected to die before morning she hung on for a couple more days. When I arrived I sat in a chair beside her bed and my brother, who was standing in the doorway, said: "You must realize that she's never coming out of the coma." "Well," I responded, "why don't you go get me a pack of 'Benson and Hedges' cigarettes, I'll stick a couple under her nose and then we'll see if she comes out or not." I thought that was hilarious but my brother only said: "I do not appreciate your humor." Mom died later that evening.

Dad soldiered on a few more years. We spent a lot of time together, on the phone, visits back and forth, a memorable Caribbean cruise. I once asked him, about a year after mom's death, if he missed her and his response was: "Not really. That little Malaysian girl's a pretty good cook." The judge had become of course a cranky, argumentative old bugger. But I more or less learned how to deal with him and could discuss pretty much anything with him from politics to economics.

At the age of ninety-one years dad decided he wanted to go on a cruise. He practically begged me to take him on a nice Caribbean cruise and my brother strongly encouraged me to agree. It was only much later that my brother admitted he would never ever have gone on any such trip with the old guy.

For the life of me I could not imagine the two of us surviving the voyage without some form of a tragedy happening. There were so many ways for it to go terribly wrong. He could have a stroke on the airplane. He could tumble down the ship's stairs or even fall overboard. He could have a heart-attack. He already had had major heart surgery. He could fall in the shower when the boat lurched. He could easily ruin three-thousand peoples' lovely family vacation. I kept wondering: how can the cruise-line allow a ninety-one-year-old guy, who is hard-of-hearing, almost blind and often spectacularly cranky, to go? I tried to talk dad out of it. I suggested he try something normal like sky-diving or bungee-jumping. Unfortunately he remained adamant.

When the big day arrived I was of course in charge of making sure we both were awake and ready for our pre-arranged taxi at 2:30 in the morning. I was so afraid of over-sleeping that I didn't sleep a wink. I just meditated, sort of, on my side of the apartment, peeking at the clock again and again until it was time. Dad was already up and the taxi was right on time. But, as we drove out of the parking-lot, dad positively freaked out. He had left his walking-cane behind. I put my hand on his arm, told him not to worry. On my way back up to the apartment, however, I was horrified to realize that I had actually forgotten our passports and all our various tickets. If dad had not forgotten his cane... I placed my head against the elevator wall and muttered: 'This is not going to go well.'

Although my stress-level was through the roof all the way along we arrived in Ft. Lauderdale without incident. In fact I learned a valuable lesson: getting through the security check is way easier when you're pushing someone in a wheel-chair. Once on board the ship I immediately settled in to literally watching every step dad took. Out of all the possible ways the trip could be terrible, however, the one factor I overlooked was dad's propensity for becoming wildly belligerent. He had a problem with everything: registration took too long, his luggage came late to the cabin, his bed was too soft, the towels were too rough.

Of course I opted for us to be seated with others at dinner rather than alone, for my sake. Everyone (else) was nice, happy, and even joyous. Dad remained silent. He was focused on his salad. We were all getting to know one another. We were all eating and talking, eating and talking. One lady, a large American woman with hair in a bun and aunt phyllis-style glasses, was especially loud and obnoxious. She went on and on until dear dad, looking up from his soup at me, positively hollered: **"You think that lady's ever gonna shut up!?"** After that I opted for us to dine alone.

One morning while waiting with a whole bunch of people at the elevator dad realized he forgot his beloved 'Bran Buds' cereal in our room. He was addicted to the stuff and startled everyone when he began wailing. "Oh for God's sake! Oh for God's sake! Oh what the hell am I gonna do?!" You must understand that we were not more than about ten paces away from our door. I put my arm around his shoulders and said: 'Dad, it's not these peoples' fault that we forgot your 'Bran Buds.' You wait here and I'll go get it."

It may have been that morning or maybe a subsequent one when, having asked him to pass the butter, dad looked up over his newspaper and remarked: "You know, the amount of butter you use, you're going to die of cholesterol." I thought about that a moment before responding: "Dad, I don't drink alcohol or smoke anything. I don't do drugs. I don't eat meat. I don't gamble and I've hardly had any sex in my entire life. Pass the fucking butter." He looked over with a wry smile and, as he slid the butter dish toward me, he said: "You're right. Here, have it you poor bastard."

The one thing dad seemed to really like, perhaps the only thing, was the classical piano music each night in the lobby before dinner. He would sit in a chair near the guy playing and pretend to conduct an orchestra, waving his hand to the music. One evening he even stood up and waved his cane around demonstrably like it was the baton, swaying with the music while everyone watched, smiled and took pictures of the sweet old man. They had no idea.

In the middle of absolutely every night I'd wake up to the sounds of dad sobbing in the bathroom. I was so tired, so over-tired in fact. I'd have to go in, talk a bit, carry him back and tuck him in. He was scared; terrified that he might pee in his bed. I assured him I'd take care of any and every eventuality. It really didn't help. He was too petrified to sleep much. Neither of us slept much. Even on that very last night I woke up to the same whimpering noises coming from the bathroom. I was really terribly exhausted by then. Like a zombie I went in, talked to him, tried to sooth him and eventually put him back to bed. Then about an hour or so later I woke up, shocked to discover that I had pissed in MY bed! I could not believe it. I was horrified.

That morning of our departure I handed the cabin boy a rather generous tip, leaned in close and whispered: "I'm so sorry but the old guy peed in his bed."

Three years later as my dad lay dying he looked up at me and said: "That cruise we went on, that was a good time wasn't it?" I agreed of course and then I thought to myself: 'You know, actually, I guess it was.'

Dad was totally lucid well into his nineties. He read 'The Globe and Mail' religiously every day even though it'd take him several hours. He was certainly not liberal in his thinking but he was sharp as a whip. His problem was not his mind. It was his body.

At ninety-three old dad still took care of his investment portfolio himself even though he could barely see. One day I heard him swearing like a sailor at his computer. He had wanted to sell some stocks but had pushed the wrong button. He mistakenly bought more of the very stocks he wanted to off-load. Of course I found that incredibly funny so he hollered at me to leave him the hell alone. Loosely translated that meant it was time to take him to Tim Horton's.

Once we were seated at Tim's with our coffees, dad proceeded to rail against everyone at his retirement home. I eventually remarked: "You know what your problem is?" "No," he said suspiciously. "What's my problem?" "Your problem is you're not senile." "What the heck does that mean?," he barked. "Well," I continued. "If you just had a little dementia happening these things wouldn't bother you so much." He looked up from his double/double and said: "Oh you just think you're so smart."

A day finally arrived when it was time to shift dad to a full-care facility. During the first week there he became quite depressed. He complained that there was nobody he could talk to. He said his spirits fell to his ankles every day and "my ankles were swollen enough before I got here." Meals were the worst times, he insisted, so I went along to see for myself. Nobody at his table seemed to talk except one lady who made no sense and a man who belted out opera terribly at the top of his lungs. My dad loved opera and hated that man. One other old man actually drooled. The nurses sat in chairs on wheels. They'd roll from one table to another and then another feeding each person a few bites in turn. Needless to say I certainly understood dad's feelings. All I could do was sympathize.

Although I talked to him every day it was a full three weeks before I could get back to Toronto. I tried to prepare myself for what was sure to be a horrible visit. Of course I immediately took dad out to Tim's and listened to all his complaints. That at least had not changed. Later, I accompanied him to the dining hall. The drooler was already in his seat, leaning precariously to one side. Dad shifted him a bit upright. "That's Morris," he told me. "He's an Auschwitz survivor." He pointed to the babbling lady and with a wry smile told me that "Sometimes she even makes sense." The opera singer shuffled in and to my tremendous surprise dad stood up to greet him. Then with arms draped over each other's shoulders, standing behind their chairs, they belted out an aria together at the top of their lungs.

Food was not served until they finished. People clapped, they sat down and then food began to come. Apparently it had become the routine. I patted old dad on his back and said: "I thought you hated the guy?" He shrugged and without looking up from his plate he said: "If you can't beat 'em join 'em."

In the end, while he lay in a coma, I sat in the darkened room alone, waiting. We assumed it was the end but not quite. Eventually I heard: "Nathan is that you?" Surprised, I sat up and said: "Yeah dad I'm still here." To which he responded: "Well why am I still here?" The old guy was already getting cranky. I quickly sat down beside him on the bed and said that I didn't know why. At that point he began to sit up. I could see his temper rising with his body as he barked: "Well who the hell knows?"

Trying to be positive I offered: "Dad, maybe it's not your time to go." He didn't like that at all. Although I had my hand on his chest coaxing him down, he raised his voice: "Don't you tell me it's not my time to go!" I kind of chuckled and said: "Dad do you really think we should argue about whether or not you're dying?" He smiled briefly, lay back down muttering softly: "You think you're so smart." Then he closed his eyes and was gone within another few minutes.

Chapter 22

Aging: The Wonderful Tragedy

A few years ago a totally hot young girl lingered after the meditation session. I knew what to do. I gave her a big hug, kissed her, turned her around and fondled her a little from behind. I could feel her body go a little limp and mould itself to mine. Then I suggested she go up to my room, get undressed and into bed but that she should make sure the lights were off before I got there. Then she smiled and asked why. I told her that I wouldn't want her to see what I look like without clothes. She said I was being silly and should come up with her but I told her I needed to get a glass to put my teeth in. That hit the mark. I asked if she played chess. She laughed nervously, said she didn't and I remarked matter-of-factly: "Well what are we gonna do while waiting for the Viagra to kick in?" Then she laughed, just laughed, not nervously. She got the picture, as I told her how beautiful I thought she was and that she really deserved a great young stud-muffin of a guy in her life. She's married now with a kid, and we're still friends.

I'm acutely aware that due to the many stories and the very nature of this book it may seem as though I've indeed been kind of a bad monk. As a matter of fact, aside from the nine months with Radha in my early twenties and a couple of months with Jaya, I've had less actual normal sex, certainly less intercourse with a 'happy ending', in forty-five years than I have fingers and toes. Actually, I should be considered an absolute expert on the effects of abstinence. But more importantly, I haven't just blindly accepted what I've been told or read about bramacharya, celibacy, the sexual component to a spiritual life or the spiritual life in general. I've watched, observed. I've tested. I've come to my own conclusions, the main one being summed up beautifully in one line by the Dalai Lama: "My religion is very simple. My religion is kindness."

While still drawing no definitive conclusions, in regard to bramacharya or celibacy, I personally have no complaints, no regrets. I've had my share of love in this life after all. I've received it and I've given it. I'm a happy guy. It's just damn lucky I know happiness doesn't correlate to the amount of sex one has in one's life. For me, this investigation is nearly over, and there are three things that have helped me become relaxed and content in that regard: meditation, old age and a prostate issue.

Gretta Vosper, a United Minister in Toronto wrote: "I want the United Church to accept that the Bible is not the authoritative word of God and that God is not where moral authority resides, and to recognize the innumerable divisions that religion has created across millennia. If they had the fortitude to say that, I think it could change the conversation of religion around the world. And that's what I'm betting on."

There's been an awful lot of chatter about god over the past couple of thousand years or so. You may have noticed. Well I have a weee problem with all of the great saints and sages, teachers and masters, past and present. I don't know what they're talking about and frankly I doubt they know what they're talking about.

Why should I believe any of them really knew or know God? If these great people wanna talk about where we come from, where we go, I can handle that. If these great leaders confine their beliefs to a universally shared underlying oneness of all life, I'm in. But God? Why should I believe any of them really knew or know what is God? I'm referring to everyone from Jesus to Muhammad, from Krishna and Ramana Maharshi or Swami Shyam to Deepak Chopra and Eckhart Tolle. I may as well offend everyone equally.

Sai Baba of Siri wrote: "There is only one religion, the religion of love. There is only one language, the language of the heart. There is only one class, the class of humanity." Up to that point I was right with him, cheering him on. But then he ends by adding: "There is only one God, he is omnipresent." Wtf? And, btw, what's with the 'he' always?

I'm a 'dhyaan yogi', a life-long meditator. That means I don't accept a philosophy, religion or any concept outside of my own direct perception. And through that process of meditation, 'samadhi', one does experience a cessation of all experience. In other words one comes to know directly oneself as the very life permeating all, pure, free. I get that. But what is that? For example, what is the state of deep sleep?

Mooji, a great teacher popular these days, says very few people in the world achieve the goal of self-enquiry, come to know the so-called true self. That of course typically implies he's one of those who has succeeded. Well, I get that as too. Through meditation the individual dissolves, like a drop of water merges with the whole ocean of life. That's great. What I have a problem with is the assumption that that is somehow akin to the concept of God. Where the heck does that ocean come from, a bigger ocean? I may be all wet but I still don't see where creation ends, or where it began. And I don't believe anyone else has either.

There's the old story of the Greek philosophy student who asks his teacher: "Sir, I understand the world is being held up by Atlas. But what's supporting Atlas?" His teacher answers: "A huge turtle." "Ok but what's supporting the turtle?" The teacher answers, slightly irritated: "Another huge turtle." "Ah, ok," says the student. Then: "But, but, what's holding up that turtle?" The teacher, out of patience, barks at his student: "Listen, it's just turtles all the way down!"

The Buddhist concept of no-self, 'shunya,' just opens the door of our minds to the reality that there's more going on than what meets the eyes. The Buddhist concept of no-self is the same in my semi-humble opinion as the Hindu all-permeating self. But what is Buddha-consciousness or nirvana? What is Brahma-vidya or moksha? What is Christ-consciousness or heaven? What is God? The enquiry must necessarily continue.

It must be of great solace to believe that somebody has all the answers: whether it be Jesus, Krishna, Ramana Maharshi, Mohammad, Swami Nityanand, Sri Yukteswar or Mooji, Aadi Shanti, Tom, Dick or Harriet. I'm not one of them. What I know through meditation after these years is that it's profoundly relaxing and freeing, that there's obviously more to 'me' than what meets the eyes and there seems to be essentially one life permeating all. I don't know God.

Another great modern day guru, Amma, wrote: "If we dive deep enough into ourselves, we will find the one thread of universal love that ties all beings together."

Meditation of course has certainly been a huge part of my life, like breathing. Meditation in fact is part of everyone's' life; only I'm quite cognizant of that fact. I've nurtured it. It's what I do. It's what I am. I'm not unfamiliar with my spirits dipping to my ankles, getting down in the dumps or dragging my ars around, so to speak. I have not escaped those times. But as everyone knows the feeling that comes with an unexpected and totally wonderful bit of news, the feeling of sheer joy filling ones chest almost to bursting, of being flushed with near ecstatic happiness, I feel that when I meditate, a lot. Is that because of the maturity of my meditation practice over all these years? Is that due to bramacharya? Personally I believe in both. A guy once asked: "Why are you celibate?" To which I replied: "For the same reason you're not. We want the same. We're just looking in different directions."

I've become one of those marginalized people you hear about on the radio, especially at Christmas time. I'm one of those people who are invited repeatedly to taverns for a turkey dinner 'with all the fixins' and for some friendly, understanding conversation. I'm one of those poor slobs that good mothers and fathers want their kids to serve food to, to teach them compassion. It has never mattered to me whether it be Christmas, New Year, my birthday, your birthday, Easter, Ramadan, Diwali or any other occasion. I've virtually always been alone, marginalized. I have always carried this feeling with me in fact for as long as I can remember, whether actually alone or not. Do I even exist? Maybe I am the tree that, should it fall in the woods nobody would hear. I have carried this feeling with me through months of silent retreats and marriage, through solitary mountain treks and morning commutes. I'm so convinced of my aloneness that it's no wonder I am in fact alone.

I'm not against the idea of going to one of those taverns in town, except that I'm a vegetarian. Also it'd be a long drive and I have enough. I'd still feel the same after food and conversation. I find it curious that the great gurus, masters and teachers actually surrounded themselves with so many people. At least those are the ones you hear about. Do they actually hate being alone? Are they actually as afraid of being alone as most everyone? Perhaps the truly enlightened ones, the ones who are really convinced of their aloneness, who know what total aloneness really is, are in Himalayan caves, Thai forest huts or Quebec vinyl-sided houses. Perhaps it doesn't really matter either way after all.

I am in fact one of those marginalized people you hear about on the radio. Only I'm as intoxicated by my aloneness and my loneliness as a person on wine. I drink in the togetherness of Christmas Eve and the peace of Christmas morning. I am in fact the patriarch sitting at the head of the table and the kid grabbing gifts from under the tree. I'm the one ladling out food at the tavern and the one gratefully eating it. I am so surrounded by family that I wish I had just one damn minute to myself and so alone that I wish I had even one family member to talk to. I am in fact both non-existent and all-pervasive.

The wonderful love of my life Radha has lived her whole adulthood in India as it turned out. We've never been friends, kept a respectful distance, even when I was there. One late night a couple of years ago meanwhile she injected herself into a dream and I clearly recall wondering why she was there. I was at my home in Wakefield. I don't recall the dream. I don't recall anything about it except that Radha was a major part and it was kinda scary. I rarely had scary dreams and that one jolted me back to the waking state. I was puzzled, even shocked by Radha's role in it. After all it was by then about thirty-five years since we'd been involved with each other. I felt shaken, even upset as I sat on the edge of the bed. Soon after, something truly amazing happened. Hardly a few hours later I received an email from my old friend Dev telling me that Radha was in Delhi and had been diagnosed with cancer. As well, I also soon discovered she had been in the doctor's office at the exact time I had the dream.

A few days later I decided to send her an email, the first ever. I wrote, "Dear Radha: Thinking of you, wishing you well." I only added that until I knew she was alright she may have to put up with the odd email from me. I never heard back, didn't expect to. I heard of course what she went through, that she eventually recovered but I continued to send an email every six weeks or so. I always wrote only: "Dear Radha: Thinking of you, wishing you well. Hansraj." Never heard back, didn't expect to. Only one time after about a year did I change my message: "Dear Radha: Thinking of you, wishing you well. Hansraj. PS; I hope you're enjoying this new connection between us at least as much as I am."

On my final visit to Kullu, face to face on the ashram steps when she had no choice but to say hello, I took her hand and asked: "Have you been getting my emails or not?" She simply took her hand back and, as she walked away she dismissively answered: "Yeah I got them." I never wrote again, don't intend to.

My urologist Dr. Adamson always seemed inordinately happy to see me. I suppose I was a little something different for the guy. He couldn't possibly have seen too many bramachari yogi/ Buddhist monk types sitting in his bland, grey-toned, window-less waiting room. He smilingly waved me into his office without even the customary announcement of my name. We chatted a minute or two before he launched into asking me the usual questions, only this time I was not willing to be dismissed as usual with the 'quality of life' speech: don't drink before bed, over-eat or get over-tired. I wanted some action.

Dr. Adamson admitted there was a new less intrusive procedure called: Transurethral Resection of the Prostate, or TURP, and he would be able to arrange it at the Gatineau Hospital where he was Head of Urology. In fact the hospital had only just recently acquired the most current state-of-the-art technology for that. But an exploratory examination would have to be done first. That could be arranged for about six weeks hence and, in the meantime, the doctor insisted I try a new pill. "I know you don't like taking pills and that they haven't worked in the past," he acknowledged. "Only these new ones are really effective with no side-effects whatsoever." I found that pretty hard to swallow, so to speak, but he insisted. "No side-effects whatsoever." I pressed him a bit further on that point until he finally offered: "Well, the only thing is you won't be able to ejaculate." My eyebrows shot up, I broke into a laugh and blurted: "Don't you call that a friggin side-effect!? I call that a side-effect!" Probably out of a sense of self defence he quickly shot back: "What do you care? You told me you don't ever ejaculate." It was of course a valid point but, as I then said, I prefer to have a choice.

Before leaving his office the doctor grinned up at me and repeated something he'd said to me on more than one previous occasion. "Nathan, you need a little pleasure in your life." As I walked out I responded: "Well it's always a pleasure to see you." Then as I made my way through the bland grey-toned, windowless waiting room I wondered if that had sounded just a little bit gay. I took the pills, for a while. As usual they didn't work and we will never know if I could ejaculate or not cause of course I never tried.

I was quite nervous on the morning of the exploratory examination. The thought of having my dick frozen and a camera stuck up it just did not sound like a wonderful way to start my day. It turned out that sitting around the waiting room in the proverbial little flimsy cotton hospital gown was at least as traumatic and in its way as painful as the examination. The good news was that there was no cancer. The bad news was, which I could've told the doctor years earlier, that the prostate was as large as a friggin pomegranate and totally obstructing the flow, and I prefer to go with the flow. So procedure was scheduled and I was left with my thoughts.

On the day of the actual operation I wasn't nervous at all. I had left a couple of fat personal checks sitting on my kitchen table, one for my former wife and one for my best friend, just in case. My papers were all in order, my 'Last Will and Testosterone' was notarized, the plants were watered, the stove was off and I'd taken a shower. At the hospital I was admitted and placed in a room, told to undress. As I lay in the bed I watched through the large window as a bright sun rose up over the city of Gatineau.

Eventually a lovely nurse came and began putting electrodes all over my chest. "What's that for?," I asked. "It's to check your heart." I smiled up at her. "It's been broken." "How did that happen?," she asked. "It was by a girl almost as pretty as you."

The End, or not.

I'm Not a Teacher, You're Not a Student (I'm Not a Student, You're Not a Teacher)

This article is written for those special people who have become interested in or perhaps even fascinated by the idea of meditation. If you're searching for instructions into a Reiki Level 1 course, Tarot cards, healing with crystals or how to contact your dead grandmother, this will not work for you. As wonderful as all those things may be, this article is exclusively concerned with explaining the pure, ancient and highly respected science of meditation, how and why to include it in your life. There is really no certification at the end of studying and practicing. There is, however, tremendous relaxation, a profound sense of well-being and a greater understanding of something rather vague I call 'self-knowledge.'

At the start of one of my sessions, a rather severe-looking lady asked what my qualifications were for teaching. A lesser man might've broken down, admitted to being a total fraud. What I said, what I always say, is that I have no certificate or accreditation from any institute. I invited her to feel free to read the back of one of my books to learn a bit of my personal history, specifically as it pertains to the study, experience and teaching of meditation. But most importantly, I added, one has to rely on one's own intellect and power of discrimination in order to choose who is worth listening to on any subject, especially this one. Moreover, ultimately, one has to take what is useful from any teacher or technique that guarantees results. Even the historical Buddha allegedly said that any technique worth employing must help a person in his or her life, here and now, right away.

One of the two main teachers in my life, Swami Shyam, once gave me a piece of advice that I continue to keep close to my heart. As I was leaving his Himalayan hermitage to join a six-month silent Vipassana Buddhist meditation retreat in Maharashtra, India, I asked if he had any last-minute words of advice. "Yes I do," he said smiling impishly. "My advice is: Don't be a Buddhist, be the Buddha." And with those words ringing in my ears I slithered away. Along with countless other words from Swamiji over the years, I've never forgotten that advice. I've often repeated it to my so-called students and even expanded upon it. Don't be a Buddhist, be the Buddha. Don't be a Christian, be the Christ. Don't be a Hindu, be Krishna. Don't be a Sikh, be Guru Nanak. Don't be a Jew, be Moses. Don't be an Asshole, be Trump.

So, no matter who we choose to listen to, sit with or learn from, it's up to each of us to dig our own freedom, to find our own way, to become the enlightened one with no certificate to show for our trouble. Just freedom. It is in the light of this realization that I humbly offer these suggestions. In reality, I am not a teacher and you are not a student. If what I write is true and if it strikes a responsive chord within you, then we are united in that understanding. We are united not as teacher and student, but as Truth itself.

Having said all that, I should add something about why it may be helpful to seek some form of guidance or a 'teacher' when beginning to examine the science of meditation. One needn't stay for long. One needn't cook or clean for him or her, do anything strange in bed or hand over one's money. What one must do is take advantage of the experience of a fellow traveler who has gone before, who has been up the path and who just might know the tricky twists and turns to watch out for along the way. And there's one more reason to sit with someone whose meditation practice has matured. The rare people who have dedicated themselves to the process over many years actually emanate a spiritual essence, a vibration that is transmitted to those around them. That may sound terribly mystical, but it's a fact and a quality not to be underestimated.

On one visit from India many years ago, my dad asked why meditation seemed to have helped me so much, but not my sister, who had also been meditating for some years. She was a devotee of a highly respected teacher, master and guru from India, Swami Yogananda, who had been a pioneer in bringing the information about meditation to the western world. Unfortunately, really, he passed away long before my sister ever heard of him. I replied to my dad that I didn't have a definitive answer to that question, assuming that he was even correct. But I offered a possible explanation. I said that if one wanted to learn to play the piano, it wouldn't really be of any use to sit in front of a photo of one's teacher placed on the music stand above the keys. Why would meditation be any different? Why, for that matter, would religion be any different? It's interesting that all truly enlightened people have said that we are one life, one energy, one love, irrespective of caste, race, creed, color or any other apparent difference. Why does the essential and original message of the enlightened beings through the ages become so perverted as to cause wars? Don't be a Buddhist, be the Buddha.

There's really nothing hard to understand about meditation. And yet, it's widely misunderstood here in the western world, and even in its home country, India. From the Sanskrit word, dhyaan, meditation has become synonymous with all things flaky and maladjusted. It's been blamed for wasted talents and even wasted lives. Nothing could be further from the truth. I will admit that I put the Saran Wrap in the refrigerator and the milk in the cupboard once in a while. But I, along with so many other people who have spent years meditating, have found something so fine, so beautiful and freeing that nothing can compare with it. Rather than blame the proud process of meditation for our foibles, we praise it as the cause of our deep sense of well-being.

My teacher, early on, once said, "Nathan, the same mind that has gotten you into trouble can get you out of it." In those days I rather hoped drugs might be the answer. But he assured me that was wrong, that drugs would only ruin my nervous system. I still prefer a mild pain-killer for headaches. However, somehow I came to understand that meditation is a powerful tool. Once trained, I realized, the mind could be used against the enemies of true happiness, such as a myriad of physical ailments, mental complexes and even the innate fear of death. Apparently, the Buddha was known to say that desires are the root cause of all problems. My mother said that lack of money is the root cause of all problems. My friend Danny seemed to think that not having many relationships is the root cause of all problems. Since I tried my mom's solution and Danny's solution for a while, I decided to try the Buddha's, even though I never actually met the fellow. I thought I saw him once at a party, but I couldn't be sure. Be that as it may, I was pretty concerned about losing my desire for money and relationships if I began to meditate. My girlfriend at the time was even more concerned. Now I see that's not how it works. You don't have to give up anything. You only have to add one thing to your life: a few minutes of meditation daily. Then sit back and watch it enhance whatever else you're into. Watch it help you let go of what you want or need to let go of. Watch it make you see the cup as half full. Watch it make you happy.

One of the most prevalent misconceptions about meditation is that you have to stop your thoughts, kill your mind. What one has to stop, cut or kill is only the concept. Leave your mind alone. To allow a wild horse to settle down, it probably isn't a great idea to put it in a very small corral. It's far more preferable to give the creature a large, wide-open field to roam around in. It'll settle down on its own. In the same way, it's far better to let the thoughts come and go freely. Merely sitting or lying down for some time each day and applying the technique assures one of a positive result. Only your misconceptions concerning what you're doing can get in the way. The very act of stopping for a while will have a positive influence on your day, your life. That's because, actually, you do not meditate. You just need to get out of the way for meditation to happen naturally. I'll explain. It's easy, yet very few people will do it.

Dhyaan actually means 'attention' or 'contemplation.' Whether a mantra (usually a Sanskrit phrase) or the breath becomes your chosen point of attention, the results of meditation, as I've said, are assured. Done with the right understanding, your mind will settle down, you will enjoy a heightened sense of well-being. Done with continuity, you will be well on your way to becoming a more contented person, walking happily through life while, of course, sometimes spoiling the milk by putting it in the cupboard.

There are three states of consciousness that everyone is very familiar with: the waking state, the dreaming state and the deep sleep state. From the moment of conception, the ancient sages have said, a person begins to forget that he or she has a fourth state, which is called Turiya in Sanskrit. This state permeates all the other states, just as water is the essence of the iceberg. So the very act of stopping all your activities and tuning in to the essence of your existence, which is what you're effectively doing in meditation, will take care of a lot. And the benefits are many.

In eastern philosophies and scriptures, you'll often read that whatever is transitory cannot be said to be real. You'll read that whatever is eternal is real and true. So this body, mind, ego mechanism is in that case not real or even existing. The ancient sages said that there is, in fact, no death because there was no birth. The space from whence 'we' come from, to where 'we' go, is considered real. The technique becomes, in the light of the previous paragraph, like an anchor. Utilizing it helps bring one's attention back to one's own self, to the reality of the essential life animating your body and mind. The technique helps us stop. As well, the technique trains the mind to focus like a laser beam, which will have far-reaching effects on your day, your life and, ultimately, your true knowledge.

The Vedantic scriptures liken the mind to a monkey flitting from branch to branch, tree to tree. Our mind flits from object to object and from thought to thought. We become so extraverted over the course of the years, or even as each day progresses, that it behooves us to find a way to regroup, so to speak. So, when we've decided to let the thoughts come and go freely while we sit and watch, we merely add one new thought. The phrase, or mantra, becomes a very significant and enjoyable thought as time marches on. All true mantras mean virtually the same thing: 'I am the pure life, the essential energy animating all the forms.' There is a popular Buddhist mantra that goes 'Om mani padme hum': 'Behold the jewel within the lotus flower.' There is a popular Hindu mantr that goes 'Amaram Hum Madhuram Hum': 'I am immortal, I am blissful and indivisible.' All real mantras basically refer to the one life, the one light at the center of all beings, the energy that animates all the forms.

It is often noted that Sanskrit is used for mantras because the vibration of the phrases resonate within the human mind to open certain spiritual channels. For an in-depth dissertation on the vibrational qualities of Sanskrit, I recommend Chaytna's book, 'Let's Learn Hindi,' which can be found through her website; www.letslearnhindi.com. I've always used the Sanskrit word; 'Shyam', as my mantra. It's the name of my teacher and of the power that sustains life. It really doesn't matter what mantra you choose, although Sanskrit mantras are the most recommended. However, choosing a mantra and sticking to it is important. Meditation is a technique of being one-pointed, after all. Chogyam Trungpa once wrote that western people tend to try many different techniques, which is like a thirsty person digging many shallow wells but never hitting water. He wrote that we should dig one well deep enough to achieve the desired result.

Having chosen a mantra, or been given one by a spiritual guide, master or guru, you're ready to begin. My teacher used to say that you should be able to meditate anywhere unless somebody is physically shaking you. I once climbed all the way down to the bottom of a dormant volcano in Hawaii, called Haliakalu, in a quest to find the perfect spot for meditation. A hut had been constructed there for trekkers or foolish folks looking for a perfect spot to meditate. I felt so sure I'd finally found my place.

Unfortunately, since there were no panes of glass nor screens in the windows, a couple of flies flew fairly frequently in there making a racket like they were at the El Macombo on a Saturday night. I left in a huff the next morning.

Later, on my way to India for the first time, I was compelled to sleep on the rooftop of a hotel in Peshawar after a long and tiring day of travel. The noise level from the crowds up there and the hollering, smoke and smells from the streets below were off the charts. I was convinced meditation would be a wasted endeavor in such a place. But, I had little choice. It was my rule to sit every evening one hour. And after an hour, in spite of my misgivings, I felt rejuvenated, refreshed. As well, contrary to popular belief, it's not necessary to sit ramrod straight with legs crossed. It's not even necessary to sit at all. You can lie down, settle into a comfortable chair or sit on a cushion with legs out or crossed. Since meditation is first a process of relaxation, let the sense of ease be your guide. You should feel relaxed and comfortable.

It's easy to find a spot where there is very little noise. It's easy to find a spot where there are virtually no pungent odors, unless of course you don't bathe. It's easy to find a spot where you're not touching anything other than the pillows. But how does one get away from one's own mental projections? As I've said before, the first thing to not do is mind your own thoughts. Don't mind your mind. Remember, the same mind that got us into trouble can get us out. The mind is a trickster, a monkey. It will first distract you from your mantra and then make you feel bad for being distracted. Allow your thoughts to come and go freely. Decide beforehand that you won't feel bad about them. Because I promise that you will be distracted again and again. So each time you realize you've been thinking or listening to a noise or feeling pain, pleasure or a strong emotion of some sort, just go back to your mantra without any sense of self-recrimination. There's no need to beat yourself up over this. You can even get right into thinking, about your day, your life. You can get into thinking about life itself, pure, free and forever. Just keep returning to your mantra, again and again.

It is important to understand that whatever one perceives and experiences in meditation, just as in ones day-to-day life, is transitory and changing. Whatever one thinks, hears, whatever pain, pleasure or strong emotion one experiences will have a beginning and an end. So, when you meditate it is useful to just watch it all. Don't try to get away from anything or hang onto anything. Just practice being the watcher of it all. The same uninvolved observer who was watching as a young boy or girl is the same one who is watching now. As your body has grown and as you've gained more and more skills, qualifications and life experiences, that watcher has never changed. That one has been watching all the changes and is watching still, unchanged, uninvolved. That uninvolved observer has always and will always be fine throughout the life and even after. Think about that.

In spite of what I wrote earlier, I am going to suggest two more techniques. Because I feel sure that the people reading this dissertation, like the people I keep meeting, and especially now with the right understanding, are brilliant enough to decide which is best suited to them and how to use the information offered here.

The first of these two techniques is called Anapana, with a soft 'a.' It is a technique of concentrating on the breath. Anapana is referred to as the maha mantra, the ultimate mantra. The reason is that it's the least tangible, the subtlest point one can attend. There's virtually no form to watch, no form to hold on to with your mind. However, the ancient sages have said that it's a bridge between the part of us that's transitory and the part that's eternal, the source of our energy. I have often suggested it can also be combined with mantr.

The million-dollar question is this: Can you allow the inhalation and exhalation to happen on its own without asserting yourself? Can you stop doing anything and just observe your own breath? While sitting, slouching or lying down, or while waiting to be wheeled in for your gall-bladder operation, put your attention on the nose-nostrils-upper-lip area and watch the breath. Don't follow your breath in or out. This is not a breathing exercise. Watch the inhalation, the exhalation and the spaces between. And, again, as often as your attention is deflected into your thoughts, the noises around you or the pain in your tummy, that many times you have to go back to your chosen point of attention. And don't bother being bothered by being bothered by being distracted.

You may not think you're having a very peaceful meditation. As I've already pointed out, you may think you're wasting your time. Just keep in mind that rooftop in Peshawar and give peace a chance. There is no such thing as a bad meditation. You may doubt that you can do it. You may doubt that you should do it. I suggest that you be patient and give yourself time. In one of my recent sessions, a lady said that she really didn't understand what she was doing while meditating. That was a valid point. It was a valid point because she was not doing anything. We're not used to stopping. We're not used to letting go. It's much simpler to run around the block for a half hour than to stop all our activities for the same time period. It's the most worthy and yet the most difficult of all activities. It's easy and hard. In fact, it's too simple. And don't get stuck on the technique. You can just watch the space, so to speak. You can decide. You are the teacher. You are the path.

Which brings me to my third suggestion, my last technique. This simple technique is close to my heart. In fact, it's close to everyones heart. Here's how this one goes:

Just think about a person you have loved with all your heart. Dwell upon that person, or even that pet, you have been most enamored of, most attached to, the being whose presence you have most treasured. Even if he, she or it is physically no longer in your life, even if the memory causes you pain, don't turn your thoughts away. The pain is because there was that much love, that much oneness and I assure you the pain and pleasure are not two different realities.

After a few moments, let go of that person or being and put your attention on the feelings, dwell on those feelings, follow those feelings to their source deep within you. Because those feelings existed long before the object of your love came in front of your eyes and other senses. Those feelings and that heart-space have always been there. Eventually, you can envision a pond that, when a pebble is tossed into it, causes ripples to spread out from the center. Let those waves, the vibrations, ripple throughout your body and flood your system with all that goodness. Envision that life-sustaining healing power spread throughout your body and even beyond. But, mostly, dwell on that place, space, center, the force, the source of your love.

One of the first things you're likely to notice is that the quality of your thoughts will change. You probably won't feel like hollering at your wife or husband so much anymore, tying a tin can to the tail of your neighbor's cat, back-ending the guy who just cut you off. You may feel uncharacteristically charitable. When that happens, and it will, you may think something is wrong. Of course, if the new thought processes seem strangely soothing, continue. It won't be long before you'll get the feeling you're looking for. When one is sitting, continuously placing ones attention on or identifying with the watcher, one is essentially developing equanimity. Each time one says 'pain' rather than 'my pain,' or 'pleasure' instead of 'my pleasure,' one is essentially stepping back from the ever-changing phenomenon just a tiny bit. In that way a person will observe again and again how all of ones sensory perceptions, whether pleasant or unpleasant, change. But a person will also observe again and again how the observer, the watcher, remains ever the same. In that way, one is travelling in the right direction and eventually, aside from any deeper effect, an ability to pause before reacting to whatever is going on around you is necessarily developed. And that ability to take a moment, even a split moment, to act creatively rather than react blindly, is incredibly valuable.

When a person throws an insult in your direction, for example, and you catch it as though it's a bouquet of roses, the insult loses all its power. It would be tempting to underestimate the technique I've suggested. But before discarding the practice out of hand to return to your Scrabble game, you may find it interesting to dwell on the fact that there are thousands of people around the world who have dedicated their lives to doing nothing else. Of course, then you'll have to figure out if they're all misguided idiots or folks who have actually discovered a way to answer first-hand those insidious questions that linger in our minds from early childhood. While everyone is striving for name, fame and fabulous wealth during this lifetime, people tend to lose sight of one very important fact. In a hundred years or so, nobody you know now will be alive. And nobody who is alive will really care who you were.

There are certain things that don't go well with meditation. Smoking cigarettes, smoking dope and drinking copious amounts of alcohol tend to be counterproductive. Heroin, crack and meth are not recommended. It's a matter of going from the grosser to the subtler. And in that regard I would also take the chance to suggest eating less meat, especially red meat, and consuming more fruits and vegetables. People who are completely into eating animals on a regular basis might not appreciate my writing that. But, I think it's really very important that I do. I only hope you don't come after me with a meat cleaver muttering something about it being all fine if you use the right spices. In fact, as i've said, nobody need necessarily 'cut' out any pleasures whatsoever. Just add one more thing to your life. Meditation will help everyone.

And while I'm offending people's sensibilities I may as well mention my belief in the importance of continence. I'm not referring to the obvious advantages of curing oneself of adult bed-wetting. After all, there are effective plastic sheets on the market these days, or so I've been told. Certainly, I'd have to be insane to suggest cutting down on sexual activity, it being the way we tend to judge how wonderful we are. So I won't go there at all. This sensitive area of the ancient science of the sages is esoteric and I therefore will not explain it. It's secret. My lips are sealed. I'm only lightly, gingerly alluding to the possibility of a certain conservation of energy. I will write all about it openly in my upcoming book, 'Unprotected Sects.'

When I returned to Canada in 1998, I was quite amazed to find out how many people had attained miraculous powers rather, well, miraculously. It still seems to me that every second person has the ability to heal merely with a touch. Many don't even need to touch you. They can do it over the phone or by skype. There are a plethora of channelers, people able to communicate with angels, crystal bowl healers, psychics, clairvoyants, palm readers, garden variety fortune tellers, intuitives, aura readers, tea leaf readers... It seems that in the new-age everybody's sister, mother and brother are powerful healers and teachers. And that's just great. I would only mention that one might be well advised to keep ones attention on the goal.

Many years ago Alan Abel, who was with the Globe and Mail in Toronto at the time, came to visit the Hermitage in Kullu, India, where I lived for twenty-five years. During his interview with My teachet, Alan asked if Swamiji had any extra-normal powers. "Yes, I do," Swamiji said. "I have the power to love everyone unconditionally." I'm quite convinced that greatest of all powers can be only attained by the direct experience of the oneness of all life, the one life permeating all the forms, pure, free and forever.

There's nothing to compel one to meditate or even make enquiries about it. However, if you've gotten this far, if you are impelled, you may as well read the rest of what I want to say. When one looks up at the night sky and sees all those stars, one has to wonder where it ends. And, for that matter, one has to wonder where it all begins. Intelligent people through the ages have continuously wondered where they came from and where they end up after the body dissolves.

I haven't an answer to those questions, not from firsthand experience or knowledge. But, I do know that asking oneself those questions is certainly the beginning of a great journey. And my direct personal experience has left me quite convinced that there is more to life than what meets the eye. There's more to me than this body and mind. This is a fact that I know through personal, direct experience. It has also become extremely obvious to me that, in spite of the many differences, we all breathe the same air, that our hearts all pulsate with the same love of life, and that we all desire freedom.

Namaste.

CPSIA information can be obtained
at www.ICGtesting.com
Printed in the USA
BVHW050342270123
656873BV00005B/14